The Fifteen Minute Miracle
Second Edition

A practical approach to
POSITIVE CHANGE

Dr. Harlan Fisher

© 2011 by Dr. Harlan Fisher. All rights reserved.

All rights reserved. No part of this book may be used or reproduced by any means, graphic, electronic, or mechanical, including photocopying, recording, taping or by any information storage retrieval system without the written permission of the publisher except in the case of brief quotations embodied in critical articles and reviews.

Balboa Press books may be ordered through booksellers or by contacting:

Balboa Press
A Division of Hay House
1663 Liberty Drive
Bloomington, IN 47403
www.balboapress.com
1-(877) 407-4847

ISBN: 978-1-4525-3756-6 (sc)
ISBN: 978-1-4525-3755-9 (e)

Second Edition

Library of Congress Control Number: 2011914398

Because of the dynamic nature of the Internet, any web addresses or links contained in this book may have changed since publication and may no longer be valid. The views expressed in this work are solely those of the author and do not necessarily reflect the views of the publisher, and the publisher hereby disclaims any responsibility for them.

The author of this book does not dispense medical advice or prescribe the use of any technique as a form of treatment for physical, emotional, or medical problems without the advice of a physician, either directly or indirectly. The intent of the author is only to offer information of a general nature to help you in your quest for emotional and spiritual well-being. In the event you use any of the information in this book for yourself, which is your constitutional right, the author and the publisher assume no responsibility for your actions.

Any people depicted in stock imagery provided by Thinkstock are models, and such images are being used for illustrative purposes only.
Certain stock imagery © Thinkstock.

Printed in the United States of America

Balboa Press rev. date: 08/15/2011

CONTENTS

ACKNOWLEDGMENTS ix

INTRODUCTION xi

CHAPTER ONE
The GIFT 1
    The Discovery of the Gift 1

CHAPTER TWO
The Phenomenon of Change 13
    Your Miracle in Progress 15

CHAPTER THREE
The Miraculous Process 17
    Like "Kentucky Fried Chicken!" 17
    The Ten "Secret" Ingredients 18

CHAPTER FOUR
A Final Secret and Hard Medical Evidence 25
    The Final Secret Ingredient – The Virus Effect 25

CHAPTER FIVE
Subconscious Thought and Beliefs 31
    Consciousness (Conscious vs. Subconscious) 31
    Belief Systems 33

CHAPTER SIX
The Learning Curve 36
    Beginning Period (1-3 Days) 37
    Positive Feelings (1-21 Days) 37

CHAPTER SEVEN
The Power of Words (1-21 days) 42
Sticks and stones will break my bones, but words will wound me forever. 42
Thoughts and Words 43
Words Activate our Intelligence! 43
Cause and Effect 44
Words are Powerful! 45
Mind and Body Connection 46

CHAPTER EIGHT
Mind Resistance as an Important Factor (1-10 days) 47
Natural Phenomenon 48
Aerobics of the Mind 49
Two Forms of Resistance 50

CHAPTER NINE
New Broadcasting (15-21 Days) 52
Concentration and Meaning (15-21 Days) 54
Create your own Program (15-21 days) 54

CHAPTER TEN
Manifesting Occurs (15-21 Days) 56
Take a Boat Trip! 58
Creating the Future! 59
Reliving the Past (18-21 Days) 59

CHAPTER ELEVEN
Designing Your Program 61
Step One—Three Choices 61
Step Two—Your Own Personal Statements 62

CHAPTER TWELVE
Statement Development 64
First Type—Affirmation Statements 64
Important Characteristics of Affirmations: 64
Common Mistakes when Writing Affirmations: 67

CHAPTER THIRTEEN
Statement Development—Types Two and Three 69
    Second Type—Positive Statements 69
    Sponsoring Words and Thoughts 70
    Triggering Devices 71
    Third Type—Instructive Statements 72

CHAPTER FOURTEEN
Last Step—Changing Who You Are 73
    Unsolicited Influence 74

CHAPTER FIFTEEN
When You Should Use the Program 76
    To Begin the Day 76
    While Driving 77
    With Exercise Programs 77
    For Subliminal Reinforcement 78
    When the Subconscious Mind Never Sleeps 79
    Using Multiple Repetition 79
    During Meditation 80

CHAPTER SIXTEEN
Conclusion 81
    Concerns 83
    P.S. The Last Surprise! 85

APPENDIX A
Programs in a Series 87
    Personal Growth Series 88
    Addiction Series 88
    Sport Series 88
    Emotional/Mental Health Series 89
    Career Improvement/Business Success Series 89
    Children's Series 89

APPENDIX B
Individual Programs For Your Consideration.......................109

ACKNOWLEDGMENTS

Like most writers, I have many people to thank—starting with the original men's group back in Las Cruces, New Mexico, all my friends and acquaintances who have used the programs, and ending with my loving wife Paula. During the last nine years these individuals have contributed valuable information that has allowed me to build, refine and understand why the process works. Without their help and continued feedback, this book and additional programs would not have been possible. My Doctoral Chairman, Dr. Morris Weinberger, challenged me to begin my quest and has since encouraged me to continue my desire to discover how and why we change.

As you will learn when you read the introduction, I also have received guidance from my inner *Voice*. This kind, understanding, and loving *Voice* has nudged me and inspired me in such a way that I have found the patience and perseverance to continue working for the last nine years to produce a final, written document. Now I am presenting this revised edition.

Paula and two of my children, Katie and Bruce, have always encouraged me as I continued to develop, design, manufacture, and complete my programs and book. Katie has consistently used my programs. Bruce has not only used various programs but has also persuaded his friends to participate in a way that has been extremely helpful to me. My skeptical son, Nathan, has forced me to question and analyze my writings and to add examples and supporting information. Paula has been an inspiration beyond words. It was her insistence that propelled me to gather all my data and begin writing. After four years, I finally have a book! Her continued editing helped me to focus on what I was trying to convey and ultimately put the words into readable form. Two other editors, Rhonda Alves and Mary Bell, contributed valuable insights about organization and clarity.

My heartfelt thanks go to all who have given me feedback and encouragement to make this final product what it is today.

I truly believe that <u>The Fifteen Minute Miracle</u> will be an asset to all who explore its message.

Introduction

I was eight years old when I first started talking with a *Voice,* and ever since that first event, we have had a continuous dialogue. Sometimes, the *Voice* starts suddenly and other times it shocks or surprises me. On many occasions it simply guides me throughout the continuous events that are occurring in my life without my even knowing what is happening. I explain more about the *Voice* in my book titled *"The Voice."* The event I am about to describe is only one of over seventy-five anecdotes presented in "The *Voice.*"

It started one evening in January 1993, as I walked into my home, the *Voice* started talking to me.

"Harlan."

"Yes, who is there?" (No answer)

"Hello, who is there?" (Still no answer)

I began to laugh at myself because once again I was surprised by the *Voice.* The *Voice* that I hear so clearly and distinctly always sounds like another person is in the room talking to me.

Then the *Voice* spoke, "Harlan, we have a lot of work to do tonight."

One of the major objectives of this book will be to help you identify all the elements surrounding the concepts that I learned that night. A lot transpired as I began to develop the programs presented to me by the *Voice.* This information has changed my life and the lives of countless others in dimensions I never thought possible. For years, I had been searching for a simple but effective way of altering and creating individual mind change. My doctoral dissertation was an attempt to determine why most beginning teachers, even after going through a four-year, certified education program, teach the way they were taught, rather than the way they were instructed to teach.

In education, we call this the "apprenticeship of observation." A large majority of new teachers do not use the new technology, teaching theories, and instructional strategies, but revert to the styles of instruction they encountered in earlier years. Of course, some new teachers do apply innovative techniques that alter children's learning behaviors. My research targeted those teachers, attempting to understand why they changed – why they used the new theories when others did not. My discovery in 1993 seemed more than an expansion of my studies. It was "a gift" given to me to share.

At the time, I thought that the approach was innovative. Today, after witnessing its successful influence on the lives of dedicated users, my beliefs have not changed. As my friend John mentioned when he read the introductory script that I prepared, "Now, I know why other programs I have used in the past have failed and why I will be successful using this approach!"

If you browse through the self-help section of any bookstore, you will notice an abundance of books related to improving your life. All the books have one thing in common; they tell you what to do but offer few materials to help you initiate the suggested methods for change. In this book, you will learn how and why the approach works and about the ten "secret ingredients" that make the program so powerful. There is also a "Final Secret" not presented in the original edition explaining The Virus Effect and Hard Medical Evidence. I will explain the twenty-one day learning curve and the byproducts of using a program. Concepts such as mirroring and broadcasting our thoughts, mind resistance, triggering devices, mind talk, mind chatter, cellular intelligence, sponsoring thoughts, virus affect, and word activation are discussed in the book.

A complete section explains how you can design your own programs. Fifteen "Power Pack Series" appear with each series containing five programs that support a central theme, such as "A Better Game of Golf," "Breaking Away from Codependency," or "Improving Mental Health." Thirty-five individual programs from which you may choose are presented. As one of my clients Chris stated, "The book offers a wealth of wisdom and knowledge that is appropriate for the general public - including children, teachers, coaches, counselors, ministers, or anyone wanting to help others change who they are."

Until you read the entire book, try to set aside your personal theories and judgments. By so doing, you will be saved the trouble of attempting to fit your ideas into what is being said. Let what you read linger passively in your mind until you are finished, for many statements that might at first bother you will become clear and acceptable in the end. You are always at liberty to believe what you wish, but remember the old saying, "a mind stretched never returns to its original form." After all, for some reason you selected this book.

As a special bonus I have included thirty-eight programs in Appendix B for you to use toward the development of your own individualized program.

Join me on a journey of self discovery. These are not motivational programs that once used the impact wears off in a few days. Rather, they are programs that are lasting, positive, and influential - something I hope you will cherish for the rest of your life.

Harlan W. Fisher, Ph.D.
June 2011

Chapter One

The GIFT

> "Harlan, we have a lot of work to do tonight"
> **The *Voice***

Have you heard the statement, "if the truth be known?" My connection with the *Voice* is a very personal one and often times will not fit societal norms. I fear that I might come across like one of those religious individuals who knock almost weekly on my door wanting to save me. Last week the new spin was "would you like our information explaining how you can be saved?"

Here is a detailed description on what happened on that night in 1993.

The Discovery of the Gift

The discovery I am about to present had its starting point in a men's group I was attending. This particular group was a Mastermind Group designed to support, mastermind or help manifest for members of the group. Masterminding or manifesting is just another way of supporting. You get involved in the listening, sharing and supporting of members of the group. Nothing shared ever leaves the group. Groups are normally no larger than six people, and the group should contain compatible group members who find it easy to support each other without serious judgment.

Feedback is very important, which comes in the form of a judgment, but not one that is a personal attack.

If you have never been a member of a support group, consider joining one. The collective consciousness of the group can create a dynamic that you cannot find anywhere else in society. Personal change will occur faster when you have other members sharing what they perceive you are trying to convey. The collective consciousness of the group creates an opportunity for whatever it is you are seeking to be manifested into reality.

The group I belonged to was a men's support group. We met weekly to brainstorm and share life experiences supporting, masterminding and manifesting for each other. One such day in January of 1993, we were sharing ideas around the concept of manifesting and affirming what we wanted through the use of positive affirming statements such as affirmations. This was an activity as part of a course we were taking, and this week's assignment was to bring to the class a series of affirmations that would support a situation in which we needed help: a better relationship, more prosperity, better career path, weight loss, or perhaps just more internal peace.

Members heard and discussed every situation you could think of, some funny, some serious, but mostly just everyday stuff. The concept of affirmations was new to most members of the group; we spent considerable time just trying to understand how an affirmation was constructed. As a starter and a point of reference affirmations are positive statements in the first person "I am"—"I have" and are always in the present tense. Present tense means that you say the affirmation as if you already own whatever it is you are asking. This is usually the concept most people do not understand.

Let's just start with some other basic understandings. I mentioned the use of "I am." Have you ever heard the statement "I am that I am?" "I am" is also the shortest complete sentence in the English language. So we will be using the "I am" to help build our affirmations and programs.

"I am an incredible person."

"I am kind and loveable."

Many benefits are associated with the use of affirmations. Wayne Dyer, a noted motivational speaker, said it best when he stated:

> "When you think positive, happy, loving thoughts, there's a different chemistry that goes into your body [from] than when you think depressing, negative, anguishing, despairing thoughts."

Wayne Dwyer is only talking about our thoughts. Affirmations are usually spoken out load, but that could be misleading. Reading something silently can be just as effective and create the same outcome. Thoughts are powerful and create energy that not only has an impact on the person thinking the thought, but also is transmitted outward and can be received by anyone. The effect we are looking for is the positive flow of energy throughout our bodies created by thinking and speaking optimistically to ourselves. Thoughts are also considered "mind talk" when you are simply talking in your mind and not verbalizing. I advocate the mental verbalization of affirmations because they have more power than when said out loud.

I mentioned the collective consciousness of the group. One thing that happens is collective thoughts are transmitted by everyone in the group. These support the individual but in a different, transmitting, communicative way.

Tape your affirmation programs!

Jeff Montgomery, a member of our group, mentioned that the best way he liked to handle his affirmations was to tape them and then simply "pop" them in his car audio player in the morning and listen to them while driving to work. I really liked this idea. I had tried several methods that seemed almost worthless for subconscious changes. For example, the common approach of writing affirmations on a card and reading them at your leisure, typically resulted in you're forgetting to take them out of your pocket and washing them the next time you did the laundry. I did this several times.

Another widely accepted approach is to write the affirmation and tape it to your bathroom mirror so that you can read it whenever you are looking in the mirror. At least you get to see this affirmation daily, unless you are out of town. Some publishing companies have developed a one a-day affirmation calendar, so that you get a new affirmation every day. In this way, you do not have to worry about writing the affirmation down. Today, you can buy computer programs that display your affirmations while you are signed on. This method may not show you the affirmations that you need for that day's problems. With these approaches, there is a limitation on the actual number of affirmations you have at your disposal.

There is the common approach of writing down your affirmations, perhaps ten or fifteen and saying them each day. This is a little better, because now you are getting involved in the writing of your own set of affirmations, which are related to your needs at the moment. These can be extremely powerful, as you will learn later.

People, who know and use affirmations, like them because they do give an instant feeling of peace and tranquility as mentioned by Wayne Dyer. Positive thoughts create positive feelings. Affirmations have this positive effect, but it is really only the tip of the iceberg, as they say.

"I am a beautiful, tranquil person."
"I am totally at peace with myself."

Being an educator, I wasn't impressed with any of the affirmation approaches I had used or explored. I knew that none of these would change, create or impact the internal subconscious long-term memory. However, Jeff's approach of recording the affirmations had possibilities. I was really drawn further, as you will soon discover. You could actually be affected by a series of affirmations that you yourself had developed and recorded. I could see using the recording over and over again and building on the program over time. Yes, this had possibilities!

I had a lot of positive desires that I wanted to manifest into my life. This sounded like a powerful, long-term approach to creating the much needed thought processes that would eventually manifest themselves into a physical form. Certainly, this could happen at a much more accelerated speed since I never felt that things were moving along at the pace I was hoping they would. The old type A personality kicked in—even though I do not consider myself a type A personality. After all, I was living in New

Mexico at the time, the land of **mañana**. Why do today what you can do tomorrow? I could not wait until that night when I would try Jeff's idea. However, I had little idea what was actually in store for me. Maybe I should have known because I had this same desire and was manifesting strongly about the potential value that could be hidden in this approach, similar to the day I discovered a lost poem in college.

I arrived home having a "knowing" that something important was about to happen. My body was alive with anticipation, but I did not know what was about to happen to me. Everything I needed to begin my taping, like Jeff had suggested, was in my living/dining room. This was a room of over 700 sq. ft. of open space with high fourteen-foot ceilings. Standing alone in that quiet room at night with the lights dimmed and the fireplace crackling, I was in a setting that seemed out of this world and a bit eerie, especially that night. I had this strange feeling that something important was about to happen. I was so excited I asked myself, "What exactly is happening to me?"

As it turned out, this proved to be one of the most enlightening, interesting, and valuable nights of my life. It wasn't just what happened but the long-term effect and impact it has had on my life ever since.

Just as I walked into the room, I heard my name called.

"Harlan."
"Yes, who's there?" (no answer)
"Hello, who is there?" (still no answer)

This time it was close to me, or at least appeared close, like it did come from within me, around me or very nearby, by but still there was definitely no one physically present in the room . . . .

I began to laugh at myself because once again I was surprised by "the *Voice*." The *Voice* was so clear and distinct that it always sounded like another person is in the room talking to me.

On this day the *Voice* said, "Harlan, we have a lot of work to do tonight."

There came the *Voice* again!

"Are you ready Harlan?"

"Yes, what do you want me to do?"

"I want you to try something new tonight, Harlan."

"Ok," I said, this time very reverent and not forceful like before.

"Together we are going to develop a unique positive affirming program."

"Thank you. That is just what I was beginning to develop."

"I know, Harlan, but this is going to have a different appeal."

"Different appeal?" I asked. "Wow, ok, I am ready to start."

"Good. First check today's mail. There is something in the mail I want you to see."

Whoa, open the mail. I thought.

"Harlan, remember I can read your thoughts, talk to me."

"Sorry, I should have known better—right!"

So I opened the big brown envelope I had received thinking if it's anything it will be in this big envelope. And it was! There was a series of affirmation programs I had ordered regarding relationships, self acceptance, self-esteem and prosperity. These were programs I had ordered from a firm that sold me some subliminal tapes. This vendor also sold the affirmation programs associated with the tape series, so you would know what the subliminal messages contained.

I was excited because here were over three hundred affirmations. When I first started writing affirmations, I had limiting thoughts as to just how many affirmations one could write using the first person present tense, yet here were over three hundred.

It wasn't a coincidence that these arrived today. What else was in store for me?

I had this feeling that, as I preceded further, everything I was going to need was going to be furnished!

Then the *Voice* said, "Harlan take these programs and come up with 75 short affirmations around the concept of relationships. Develop a relationship program from these four sets of programs you have received."

I asked, "What do you mean by a program?"

"A program is a series of supporting affirming statements around a central theme. The theme, in this program, will be relationships, but this theme will contain self-acceptance issues, self-esteem issues, prosperity issues and much more. Be creative, I will help you."

I began reading the affirmations, marking those I liked. Soon I had a series of seventy-five affirmations that were short and supported each other through the theme of relationships. It was not difficult at all. It seemed that as I read the perfect affirmations, they just jumped out at me and said take me—I did. It only took a matter of minutes.

"But why just 75 affirmations?" I asked.

"This program will only be fifteen minutes long. I want you to record the affirmations with little inflection. Be clear in your speech, leaving a space between each affirmation, so that tomorrow you can say that same affirmation in the space you provided."

"Wow, I said, this is audacious." I was trying to be humorous, because I was talking with the *Voice,* still having trouble realizing what was truly going on and knowing that it did not matter. I was getting all the help I needed to develop this program.

The *Voice* went on to say, "Let's get some good background music to go with the program. You have the music of the Fairy Ring Angel's, right next to the recorder.

"Great idea," I said, and sure enough there was the tape. I was going to ask how the tape got there but just smiled. It was beautiful music, and absolutely the right choice. Truly it was. If you ever get an opportunity to listen to the music "Fairy Ring" you will know what I mean.

"I thought you would like it," the *Voice* said."

I wondered if the *Voice* was smiling, like I was.

And so I started. It was incredible. I said the affirmations, making sure that I had the proper length of time between each affirmation. To determine the length of the pause, I repeated the same affirmation, except I was silently lip reading. During the space between the affirmations, I slowly moved the microphone toward the music. I stopped the recording production several times, to check the volume on both recorders, making sure they were of the same noise level.

That was pretty much it. I finished the program in a very short period of time—only about twenty minutes, and used close to the 75 affirmations.

And then puzzled, I remembered asking the question, "why only fifteen minutes?"

The *Voice* came back and answered with a question, "what is the normal attention span of an adolescent or adult that will be using these tapes?"

"Thirteen to eighteen minutes. Oh I see. This is an average between these areas to ensure catching the prime attention span of both."

"That's correct Harlan," the *Voice* commented."

"What do you mean about others using these programs?"

"You will be sharing these with others."

"These? But I am only making one."

"There will be others Harlan."

"Oh, ok! I mean why question, right? Others, ok I'm going with the flow. Lead on."

"Not tonight Harlan, we have a lot of work to do before further developments."

I thought, *more programs*! I was too excited about this one to question any further.

I listened to the program again. Only this time, I actually used the program, as designed, and said each affirmation verbally in the space I had provided. When I finished, I played it again, and again.

It was fun and interesting to hear myself saying my own affirmations. It allowed me to say each affirmation with enthusiasm, different inflections, tonal quality, sing them, add to them and just have a ball creating and making the affirmations personal.

This was incredible, and I was so amazed at what had just been created. Wait until the others see this tape creation.

"Thank you."

"You are welcome, Harlan. Just one more thing: for these tapes to be highly affective, I want them used consistently for twenty-one days."

"Twenty-one days?"

"Yes Harlan, what can happen in twenty-one days?"

"That same approach—a question for a question." *The Voice should have been a lawyer,* I thought.

"Harlan, please. Lawyers are people just like you."

"Whoops! Sorry, I forgot we could communicate by thought."

I thought about the question. It took me a while to answer, but it appeared that the *Voice* wanted me to come up with the answer . . . . Ah, yes. Remember that we can break or develop a new habit in twenty-one days using this approach, right. I learned this, years ago, in a management-training program designed to draw customers. (Notice how the *Voice* asked me the question for which he knew I had the answer. I was simply being led to discover my truth, the truth I already knew).

"Right Harlan—you have done a good job. But remember this is just the beginning."

"Ok, thank you too."

Then, I think the *Voice* went to bed, because that was our last conversation that night. Sorry, just trying to add some humor to what had just happened. Whew!! What an evening.

A New Beginning

This whole production only took a little over two hours. I realized what I had just completed—only about the most powerful learning tool I had ever seen in my over sixteen years of practicing education. I should probably count the nine years I spent getting my four education degrees or a total of some twenty-five years. Why it is so powerful is explained more fully in my book "The Fifteen Minute Miracle." However, I am presenting the ten secret ingredients in the next chapter so you too can see why this was such a fantastic discovery.

Understand that together the elements used created a harmonic learning balance bringing about key intense learning moments. Educators love to discover these types of learning moments. Beautiful isn't it? The use of powerful affirmations, the subject matter correlation, the music, the length of the program and the twenty-one day theory all contribute to one of the most powerful fifteen-minute learning tools I had ever seen.

I couldn't wait until morning. I started calling members of my support group to share what had happened. I asked for a meeting the next night to show and play the program. I stayed away from the whole story about how I got help with the creation and direction. I wanted to explain this to them face to face.

Why had I not heard about this approach and, why was it so simple? I thought that it was too simple, but most of the time, the simplest principles can create the most dynamic outcomes. Have you ever heard of the KISS principle? This is a phrase often used in educational circles to imply—"do not make it difficult. Learning occurs easily and simply." KISS means "Keep It Simple Stupid."

Imagine receiving an incredible Gift from your *Voice*, as I did back in 1993. Since this first discovery, nothing has ever been changed from what was first developed. It was that perfect. The process put me into a different state of mind. Here is what it can do for you.

Raising the frequency level of your Energy Vibrations

The simple fifteen-minute programs put you into a higher level of thought, which is vibrating at a much higher level of energy frequency than normal. This alone puts you into a euphoric mood, giving you that feeling of well being, which was described by the users of the programs. At least for a period of fifteen minutes you will have the ability to lift yourself to these higher levels of energy frequency necessary to transform yourself into this ecstatic state of well being. At this point, you are much more apt to deal with solutions to many of your life's issues related to mental health, sports, career, family, relationships with others and addictions and put you in a position to begin to access your *Voice*.

Feelings vibrate, just as all things in the universe do, at a particular frequency. Negative feelings like anger, guilt, and depression vibrate at low frequencies, while positive feelings like joy, appreciation, and passion vibrate at high frequencies. These high frequency vibrations make us feel good. This is why people and places that inspire and cultivate positive feelings have what we call higher or good vibrations; these ultimately lead you to tap into your higher self and hear the *Voice*.

In addition, higher vibrations inspire health, happiness, and optimism. When we are tuned into good vibrations, our bodies heal, our hearts open and our minds shift toward higher vibrations, such as the *Voice*. It is when we reach these higher frequencies within, that we begin to see new possibilities and feel powerfully energized to follow our inner higher self, the *Voice*. Higher vibrations put us in a state of perfect receptivity so that we feel it is the energy flowing through us that accomplishes what needs to be done. We feel guided, supported, protected, and nourished when we are in this flow. You will cherish these feelings so much that you will want to feel that way all the time. When we are receiving and sending out powerful higher vibrations, we are always in the flow.

Further, having thoughts of shame, fear, craving, anger, and pride are all going to weaken you. Positive thoughts strengthen you because they are higher levels of vibration. For example forgiveness is 350, reason and understanding 400, love is 500, and peace at 600 is the highest we will ever reach. While having these thoughts, you are most apt to talk to or hear the *Voice*.

Chapter Two

The Phenomenon of Change

Years ago, I read an old Chinese proverb stating:

Tell me and I forget;
Show me and I remember;
Involve me and I understand.

Memory of the proverb influenced the creation of the program about which this book is dedicated. The program employs every component necessary for successful learning and change. The strategy "tells" you, "shows" you, and finally, "involves" you. The short, simple technique brings together all the necessary elements, creating a harmonic learning balance. Because I have spent twenty-five years in the field of education—nine years obtaining my four degrees and sixteen years as a practitioner—I was thrilled when I began to realize the power of the process. Like all educators, I love to discover effective teaching strategies, and like all psychologists, I love to find new ways to help people.

The importance of the program was highlighted one evening when my wife and I were watching a television program about the life of Tiger Woods. During the early part of the movie, young Tiger, somewhere around his tenth birthday, went into his bedroom, plopped down on his bed, put on his audio headset, and started listening to a tape. He was using affirmations. He would say a positive, affirming statement around the concept of golf, like "I am a great golfer;" "I have a perfect swing;" "I stay calm, cool, and collected."

My wife and I looked at each other in amazement because this was very similar to the programs I developed in 1993. At first, my recordings included numerous subject matters surrounding our lives, such as relationships, self-acceptance, forgiveness, and health. During the past year, I have developed more recordings on such things as golf, business, basketball, confidence, anxiety, depression, healing your body and mind, and divorce.

Stephen Covey's book, <u>The 7 Habits of Highly Effective People</u>—an international bestseller—emphasizes the importance of a positive, mental attitude. Some of his philosophies are expressed in inspiring maxims, including "Your attitude determines your altitude;" "Smiling wins more friends than frowning;" "Whatever the mind of man can conceive and believe, it can achieve." Covey's leadership center and books focus on empowering people to take control of their lives, just as Tiger Woods learned to do at an early age. We can all agree that Tiger Woods has strong inner confidence and is one of the greatest golfers of our time. The taped program he used as a child certainly helped him develop the qualities which we admire in him as a golfer. Sports commentators continually remark on how he stays so poised under pressure and remains so consistent.

Mother Theresa of Calcutta, one of the most respected spiritual leaders of the Twentieth Century, deeply affected the world. Those who knew her realized that she developed much of her positive attitude through prayer. At twelve she felt her first desire to devote her life to God's work. She prayed and discussed the idea with her sister and mother. She asked her father, "How can I be sure?"

He answered, "Through your joy. If you feel really happy by the idea that God might call you to serve Him . . . then this is the evidence that you have a call. The deep inner joy that you feel is the compass that indicates your direction in life." Hence, she dedicated her life to helping mankind.

The world-champion boxer Muhammad Ali told everyone, "I am the greatest!" When he affirmed his greatness or stated that he was going to do something spectacular, he almost always did exactly as he said he would do. He continually declared, "I will put him out in the fourth round—he will never touch me—I am the greatest."

These individuals, in spite of the pressures of the world, have demonstrated the ability to develop great skills and become masters of their own lives. Many others seem to let life confuse and overwhelm them, they seem lost and helpless, and their lives drift as in a storm-swept sea. The difference can be traced to choices and a definite positive way of thinking. Louis Hay explains in one of her affirmations about accepting responsibility for our actions and choosing to make appropriate changes:

In the infinity of life where I am,
all is perfect, whole and complete.
I now choose calmly and objectively to see my old patterns
and I am willing to make changes.
I am teachable. I can learn. I am willing to change.
I choose to have fun doing this.
I choose to react as though I have found a treasure
when I discover something else to release.
I see and feel myself changing moment by moment.
Thoughts no longer have any power over me.
I am the power in my world. I choose to be free.
All is well in my world.

Your Miracle in Progress

Do you feel like you are in a rut, stuck and want to change? Would you like to program yourself like successful people? If you knew how, would you be willing to experience inner peace, happiness, health, success, or whatever you want in life? At this moment, ask yourself what you want that you do not have.

The next chapters illustrate how to reach your goals and describe in detail a way to achieve the same assured, self-confident attitude of Tiger Woods, Mother Theresa, and Ali. What we believe and what belief systems we hold deep in the recesses of our subconscious minds influence every experience in our lives. Positive programming is something we all need, regardless of our life endeavors.

Change is simple but not effortless

There is nothing magical about my approach because change is a simple process and can be accomplished under the right conditions. In fact, my grandmother used to say, "The only thing constant is change." So do not look at your life changes as difficult or complicated. Change, however, is not an effortless process. It requires you to be willing, informed, and tenacious. The trick is to follow a path which will enhance the quality of your life. My book and programs will help. They are unique—a one of a kind-format. The very simplicity of the approach has eluded even the best of minds over the years. When I asked my friend Rae why she liked the program, she stated, "It is so simple it works." It is a method that helps you change using an easy process.

Chapter Three

The Miraculous Process

> "The *Voice* told me I was special. I was also assured that I had a gift and a purpose."
> **Dr. Harlan Fisher**

Like "Kentucky Fried Chicken!"

When my wife first saw what I had created, she commented that my technique reminded her of "Kentucky Fried Chicken." Asked what she meant, she replied that like the recipe for the Colonel's chicken, if we were to take one element out of the program, it would not be "special." Take one ingredient out of the preparation of the chicken and not only is the chicken ordinary but also the Colonel is out of business.

Although simple—my technique will not work if the process is not followed.

To insure *optimal, learning moments*, the user must employ all of the ingredients to achieve the desired outcome. Leaving out just one of the ingredients alters the formula, and users will not receive the full impact of what the series is capable of accomplishing. A total of ten "secret ingredients" are necessary for change.

The Ten "Secret" Ingredients

The Design

The first secret ingredient is the orchestration of the program. The design actually captures the attention of the listener in a new and unique way, therefore creating an important learning event. The "listen and say" approach, in which a person hears the short statements and then repeats them, captures attention and focuses the user's thoughts on the task at hand. You rarely lose your focus unless you stop the program.

Intense focus helps create internal awareness, the first key to promoting an attitude necessary to begin subconscious programming. Since the statements are always positive, you are forced into an optimistic state of awareness. Continued use of the programs will eventually lead the subconscious to more self-enhancing, positive behaviors and beliefs.

Awareness must be present before thought evolves or is activated. The mind transforms stimuli into thoughts of infinite possibilities. If compatible information already exists within the mind, programming becomes easier. However, if the information is contrary to what exists within the structures of the mind, resistance occurs, thus creating a different scenario. I will talk about mind resistance in more detail in a later chapter.

Your awareness stimulates thoughts that are capable of generating new mental impulses, which in turn create new biological information. Because the design of the program utilizes a structure that guides you to a higher level of learned patterns, you are one step closer to changing the "world of your mind."

What comes next isn't surprising. Our minds are challenged and energized, not in static way but in a flexible, dynamic manner. We have created the necessary ingredient for synergy—cooperation between all elements of the mind. When a high level of synergy exists, the ability to change the direction of thoughts occurs quickly. In other words, we cope more easily with the new information necessary to alter thought patterns.

We possess established thought experiences that lock our minds into predictable patterns. Many of these patterns are beneficial and necessary, but some are detrimental. Entrenched and damaging thought patterns keep us from growing or changing. All the early programming fed to us by our parents, siblings, grandparents, and others amount to over 25,000 hours, embedded within our minds. Such conditioning continues unless we take steps to alter prior beliefs. Use of affirming programs will challenge negative, ingrained ideas of the past and push the mind to accept new and vital energy forces.

Seventy-Five Statements

Secret ingredient number two is the introduction of 75 centrally focused positive statements. Each program revolves around a theme such as self-esteem, self-acceptance, relationship, or prosperity. Every statement builds on the theme, allowing the mind to accept more readily what is being introduced during the process. Compared to writing a random page of nice affirmative statements, the continuity insures focus and concentration, some of the key requirements for an ultimate learning moment.

The program concept expands beyond one central theme to a series of supporting taped recordings called Power Pack Series. One example is the theme, An Independent, Self-Determined Life, with supporting tapes, "It's Okay to Be Me," "Forgiveness," "Recovering from Addictions," "Setting Boundaries," and "Living your Dreams."

Building Your Own Program

Secret ingredient number three allows you the liberty to personalize the statements. This ingredient occurs around day fourteen or fifteen of continued use of the programs. When the opportunity presents itself, the user begins to elaborate on what is being said, making the programs more personal and more powerful. A positive statement like, "I love and care for myself," can be altered to "I, Harlan Fisher, love and care for myself every moment of the day." Using the individual's name personalizes the statement, and the mind hears and responds accordingly.

The Power of Your Voice

Secret ingredient number four occurs because our voices are powerful tools. In this case, the voice helps to maintain concentration. In order to repeat a statement, we must hear it first. Our attention is always focused, contributing to a high learning curve. The voice, when used properly, creates an emotional tone to the program by the way we speak a phrase, thus supporting the old adage, "It is not what you say that counts but how you say it."

Verbalizing the statements contributes to the total outcome by allowing personal expression, and as a consequence, producing an impact on the mind. Some psychologists use this approach. It is especially effective with patients suffering from situational depression. The psychologist directs the individual to look in a mirror and say kind, loving statements. Many times, the act shocks people into reality, steering them away from negative, controlling thoughts.

When you hear positive statements in your own voice, the psyche receives the commands and integrates them appropriately. Because words are a powerful, creative force, persons talk to themselves and use verbal or mind-talk commands in response to the world. Often, the internal messages are negative and counterproductive—words of discord, fear, limitation, or low self esteem. To create a positive world, you must reinforce the positive attitudes—joy, success, love, energy, self worth, or responsibility. By concentrating on positive commands or affirming statements, you release your higher self. You will convince your mind by addressing it in a variety of tones. Eventually, the mind will start to believe what you are saying. For instance, try shouting the statements, singing them, stating commands, or using a persuasive voice. Experiment! After all, it's your mind you are trying to convince.

Through the directional nature of the programs, you are able to create stronger, more assertive methods to influence the subconscious mind. By employing self-direction and voice power, you establish new beliefs in the same, natural way that your subconscious mind has always learned. You will say the positive statement, feel the power of the statement, and experience an emotional response. Finally, the statement becomes your personal command.

Mind Chatter

Secret ingredient number five is the elimination of mind chatter. Mind chatter is akin to mind talk, which I mention throughout the book. Mind talk and mind chatter are different because with mind talk, we control what we are thinking; we deliberately think about an idea but do not verbalize it. Mind chatter happens when we are thinking about or doing one task, and other notions interfere, rapidly running through our mind. The design of the program eliminates mind chatter and focuses the user's attention on the task at hand. The control of mind chatter is a critical factor in reducing the number of times you have to hear, do, or say the ideas.

Only Fifteen-Minutes Long

Secret ingredient number six, the fifteen-minute length of the program, also contributes to the learning outcome because by the time the mind tires and mind chatter interrupts concentration, the program has reached its conclusion. Therefore, ultimate programming has occurred. Some educators contend that the attention span is as short as nine seconds. They claim that if you are working with a curriculum that doesn't get you involved or say something that arrests your attention every nine seconds, you begin to daydream and your mind wanders. My technique fulfills both beliefs:

(1) it lasts only fifteen minutes, and
(2) it gets you involved every few seconds.

Simplicity of any learning strategy contributes to maintaining attention. Use of individual words, short phrases, and simple sentence structure promotes concentration. The statements should be approximately six to eight words but may include more, depending on their impact. The train of thought must stay on one, concentrated track.

I have often told friends that Dr. Gerald Mann, minister at Riverbend Church in Austin, Texas, would not be considered such an outstanding speaker if his sermons lasted over eighteen minutes. One day, I saw him in a television interview, being questioned about sermon length. His response was exactly as I had predicted. He acknowledged that if he extended his talks, he would lose much of the audience. He wisely keeps his sermons between fifteen to eighteen minutes. I have listened to many speakers with delivery as polished as Mann's, but who lost the audience after twenty minutes. Heads began to nod, some individuals dozed off, and others started looking around or talking to break the monotony.

I know of another minister who was repeatedly told that his sermons were too long, but he would not listen. He was a truly gifted orator but talked more than forty-five minutes. Church service would last more than an hour and a half, even though it was scheduled to stop in one hour. People would get up and leave, yet this did not stop the minister from continuing. His church no longer exists, while Dr. Gerald Mann's church has grown to be one of the largest in the Central Texas area.

You may have attended a lengthy class lecture in high school or college. You tried to take notes but found yourself wiggling, turning, talking, and doing whatever necessary to avoid the "pain" of trying to make your mind listen to the subject being presented. British historian and lecturer Arnold Toynbee commented:

The mind will tolerate only as much as the seat will bear.

Consequently, a key to my program is to break up the subject matter intermittently with listening and speaking activities that result in a fifteen-minute participation series. Many self-help or motivational programs on the market are merely too long and the optimal goal is never achieved.

Simplicity

Secret ingredient number seven is simplicity, another key strategy to the success of the program. The statements are not complicated, but short and concise, making the program easy to use, say, and follow. When you first use the programs, they actually look too simple to work—but do not be fooled. As one client named Jane told me, "The power is in the simplicity. I can work the program into my busy schedule and make the changes that I most desire."

Twenty-one Times/Twenty-one Days

Secret ingredient number eight applies the twenty-one times or twenty-one day principle. Twenty-one repetitions are universally recommended for creating a new habit. Matthew McKay and Patrick Fanning in <u>Self-Esteem</u> (second edition) state that in order for any behavior to become automatic, the routine must be repeated over a period of twenty-one days. Both Essi Systems (committed to the transformation of workplace stress) and Smoke

Stoppers (helping people to quit smoking) promote the 21-day rule for behavior change.

Accordingly, I recommend the use of my program for twenty-one days. If you forget for a day, you add two days to the program to compensate for the interference with the learning curve and to provide the necessary reinforcement. Additionally, you must actively use the series as prescribed at least once a day. Then, if you wish, you may passively listen to the program to reinforce the desired results. For some reason, which we yet do not understand, too much use of the program does not enhance the possibility of quicker success. However you use it, the following two factors must NOT be altered:

(1) **a**ctive participation in the program once a day, and
(2) repetition of the program for at least twenty-one days.

Just as a physician recommends that the full course of antibiotics must be completed to insure recovery, so do I insist that the program be completed as prescribed.

When a stressful situation threatens to cause you to relapse into old habits, you should use the program as an opportunity for support. For instance, an athlete may begin use of the golf series before an important tournament. The dating program may be used if you are apprehensive about an upcoming date. Since all of the tapes have an uplifting effect, I recommend you keep at least one tape at your disposal all of the time. The strategy reinforces positive thinking and puts you in a better frame of mind.

Easy Repetition

Secret number nine creates easy to use, repetitious statements in such a way as to highly impact the subconscious mind. A seventy-five (75) statement program heard and repeated actually amounts to one hundred and fifty (150) repetitions in a fifteen minute period. The impact occurs by hearing the messages, repeating the messages, and using subliminal messages. Many people do not understand subliminal messages, so I have included a section in the book on the subject. Subliminal messages occur in our daily lives even though we are not aware of their significance.

Music

Secret number ten includes soothing music to enhance a mood conducive to learning. Music allows the listener to use the tapes in prayer and meditation, as well as for a learning tool. A good time to passively experience the program is just before going to bed. Since one recording is only fifteen minutes long, it will not disturb you if you drop off to sleep—it will simply shut itself off while the mind continues to absorb.

Chapter Four

A Final Secret and Hard Medical Evidence

The Final Secret Ingredient – The Virus Effect

I could call this *Secret number eleven* but it was actually discovered once I did research on the people using the programs. I call it the **Virus Effect**. Once you change just a little part of your thinking processes, the simple changes begin to spread and influence your total thought processes, just like the spreading of a virus. Soon, you will find that you are beginning to think and act in a more positive manner. Your friends will begin to comment on how much you have changed. As mentioned, when you begin to reach a higher positive level of thinking, you begin operating at a higher energy frequency, and it becomes much easier to communicate with the *Voice*.

If you repeat the phrase, "I like myself," for fifteen minutes a day for twenty-one days you will create this virus effect. Here is where the virus affects the rest of your thoughts. The "I like myself" becomes, "I like myself at work," "I like myself as a person," "I like myself as a father or mother," "I like myself as I am," and on and on. The virus effect of "I like myself" begins to transfer into extended thoughts like the ones I just mentioned. This was an incredible finding and one that is quite useful. Actually, we found that just one fifteen-minute program on any subject began to change the individual's life dramatically in all different dimensions.

There is also a connection between the way you think and what you believe about the world. Your reaction is independent from what you think about. Negative thoughts lower your energy field; positive thoughts empower you. You are literally disempowering yourself every time you have a negative thought. Everything is energy and what we think about impacts our physical body. As the saying goes, what you think about expands and manifests itself in the physical world. See how powerful positive programs can be, especially if they are actually programs around a central theme like self acceptance, relationships, career, happiness or any of the other areas of your life you want changed. We need to change the way we vibrate so that we can put ourselves in harmony with others who are vibrating at a higher level.

Most of the experiences in our life are low-level frequency events, such as anger, fighting, etc. People cannot be in internal conflict when they are operating at a high level of frequency. Try to avoid any conflicts in your life. Conflicts are a violation of harmony. These decrease your chance to reach that universal higher energy level, the *Voice*. The moment you cease to hate and instead bring love into the mix, your whole life changes. Move out of the energy of fear and hatred, thereby relieving you of the influence of negative thoughts. You cannot be sad and joyous at the same time. The one is opposite of the other; therefore, keep joy in your life by thinking positive thoughts.

All matter is made up of energy, and that energy is in motion continually. Everything in the universe, from the smallest molecules to the most complex living beings, has an optimal rate of vibration. Thoughts, emotions, intentions, choices, and actions contribute to our vibration state. Affirmative activities that leave us feeling joyous, appreciative, loving and peaceful raise our vibration. A positive outlook, created by the process presented, becomes the most important tool you possess. This outlook will sustain you when the path leading toward transformation is wide and winding. As you continue to evolve, your vibration frequency will also evolve, aiding you in the creation of an even higher reality that ultimately will lead you to your higher energy self, the *Voice*.

This is a Special Chapter not presented in the original edition of *The Fifteen Minute Miracle*.

Are you wondering if Affirming Positive Statements work?

Hard Scientific Evidence

Hard scientific evidence, proof, exists that positive thoughts can shape your life.

Current trends in neuroscience offer <u>evidence</u> that we can consciously improve our health and wellbeing by simply changing our thoughts. "Discoveries in 20th century neuroplasticity have demonstrated that the physical reality of our brain has been formed from our past experiences and can change based on new input," says Danea Horn (<u>Affirmations—The Science Behind Why They Work</u>). Here is a little of what she has to say:

Change Your Life

"The experiences in life are in large part determined by individual beliefs . . . Constant repetition creates and strengthens connections in our brain. For instance, if you were told, over-and-over again, that you were poor, you would have physically created connections in your mind to reinforce the belief of being poor. You would have habits that supported those beliefs and a resulting reality of being poor.

However, just as the musicians with focal hand dystonia, we can rewire our brain, the actual physical connections in our brain, by introducing and repeating new life affirming beliefs. Affirmations repeated continuously, can create new neural connections, that in a very real physical sense, change our physiology and support new habits and behaviors that can change life.

We do not have the brain of our youth. Our brains, not just our minds or our thoughts, but our actual physical brains are in flux and responding to our environment and sensory input continuously. This is where we get our mind power."

Lauren Robins, (MS, LMT) in the article <u>The Indefinite Body</u> says, "Thoughts create chemicals that pour into the rivers and streams coursing through our body. Within 20 seconds, the chemical composition of the body is altered by a thought, having an acid or alkaline effect on our body . . . As we persevere on limiting negative thoughts, our nervous system sends chemicals to muscles; our physical body contracts and thinking becomes foggy."

Cathy Chapman, Ph.D., LCSW, a licensed clinical social worker writes in <u>Strengthening the Immune System</u>: "If you are someone who thinks sad, angry or negative thoughts most of the day, you are weakening your immune system. The chemicals in your body which fight off infection can be clinically shown to decrease."

Dr. Joseph Dispenza in <u>Physics, the Brain and Your Reality</u> says: "The thinking brain, the neo cortex, is the seed of our freewill and allows us to have a choice and opinion. The one thing I noticed about people who had changes in health had changed their thinking. If they changed their thinking, was the effect in the brain sending a new signal to their body? The answer is yes . . . Our thoughts have a direct connection to our direct level of health. Thoughts make a chemical. If you have happy thoughts then you're producing chemicals that make you feel happy. If you have negative thoughts, angry thoughts or insecure thoughts, those thoughts make chemicals to make you feel how you're thinking . . . There is sound evidence that our thoughts do matter. We always replace those old patterns with a greater ideal of ourselves. If rehearsed mentally, we will grow new circuits in the brain, the platform in which we stand on to execute a new level of self."

Dr Joseph M Carver, PhD, in the article <u>Emotional Memory Management: Positive Control Over Your Memory</u> writes, "Thoughts change brain chemistry. That sounds so simple but that's the way it is, with our thoughts changing neurotransmitters on a daily basis. If a man walks into a room with a gun, we think 'threat,' and the brain releases norepinephrine. We become tense, alert, develop sweaty palms, and our heart beats faster. If he then bites the barrel of the gun, telling us the gun is actually chocolate, the brain rapidly changes its opinion and we relax and laugh—the joke is on us . . . We feel what we think! Positive thinking works. As the above example suggests, what we think about a situation actually creates our mood. Passed over for a promotion, we can either think we'll never get ahead in this job (lowering serotonin and making us depressed) or assume that we are being held back for another promotion or job transfer (makes a better mood)."

Dr. Caroline Leaf, a brain researcher from South Africa with over 25 years in this field, says in <u>Thought Life</u>: "87% to 95% of the illnesses that plague us today are a direct result of our thought life. What we think about affects us physically and emotionally. It's an epidemic of toxic emotions... The average person has over 30,000 thoughts a day. Through an uncontrolled thought life, we create the conditions for illness; we make ourselves sick! Research shows that fear, all on its own, triggers more than 1,400 known physical and chemical responses and activates more than 30 different hormones. There are INTELLECTUAL and MEDICAL reasons to FORGIVE. Toxic waste generated by toxic thoughts causes the following illnesses: diabetes, cancer, asthma, skin problems and allergies to name just a few. Consciously control your thought life and start to detox your brain!"

Neuroscientist <u>Helen Mayberg</u> did not endear herself to the pharmaceutical industry by discovering, in 2002, that inert pills—placebos—work the same way on the brains of depressed people as antidepressants do. Activity in the frontal cortex, the seat of higher thought, increased; activity in limbic regions, which specialize in emotions, fell. She figured that cognitive-behavioral therapy, in which patients learn to think about their thoughts differently, would act by the same mechanism. (Read more in <u>How Thinking Can Change Your Brain</u>)

Dr Joe Dispenza explains in *What the Bleep* that where the neurons of the brain connect, they integrate into a thought or a memory and that these thoughts are organized by association into a thought pattern, or "neuro-net." He illustrates this by explaining, "*The concept of and the feeling of love for instance is stored in this vast neuro-net. But we built the concept of love from many other different ideas. Some people have love connected to disappointment; when they think about love, they experience the memory of pain, sorrow, anger and even rage. Rage may be linked to hurt, which may be linked to a specific person which then is connected back to love.*"

He says that physiologically that *nerve cells that fire together wire together.* If you practice something over and over again, those nerve cells have a longstanding relationship.

"If you get angry on a daily basis, if you get frustrated on a daily basis, if you suffer on a daily basis, if you give reason for the victimization in your life, you are re-wiring and re-integrating that neuro-net on a daily basis and that neuro-net now has a long-term relationship with all those other nerve cells called an identity.

We also know that nerve cells that don't fire together no longer wire together; they lose their long-term relationship because every time we interrupt the thought process that produces a chemical response in the body, every time we interrupt it, those nerve cells that are connected to each other start breaking the long-term relationship. When we start interrupting and observing, not by stimulus and response and that automatic reaction, but by observing the effects it takes, then we are no longer the body-mind-conscious-emotional person that's responding to its environment as if it is automatic." (Emotional Chemistry)

Deb Shapiro, the bestselling author of *Your Body Speaks Your Mind*, says that there is now a whole new science called pschonueroimmunology exploring the relationship between the psyche or mind, the nervous system and the immune system. He asks if you ever wondered how the power of your thoughts can affect your body? He gives the example of Dr. Bernie Siegel, the author of *Love, Medicine and Miracles*, who was giving a talk to a room full of skeptical doctors when he brought out a copy of *Lady Chatterly's Lover* and proceeded to read the most erotic part. As he put the book down he said, "Just as reading a book can stir our sexuality, so you can see how our thoughts and feelings can affect us physically." The doctors were immediately convinced.

A study in the journal *Science* finds that an affirmation exercise improved the grades of African-American middle school students, and the effects lasted for at least another two years after the test period according to author Geoffrey Cohen, an associate professor of psychology at the University of Colorado at Boulder. When children write about their values, these self-affirmation exercises can help boost grades, new research suggests. (Read more at Affirmations Improve Student Grades)

The *Voice* was right; these programs are special and can change our lives in dimensions we never thought possible.

Chapter Five

Subconscious Thought and Beliefs

The possibilities of creative effort connected with the subconscious mind are stupendous and imponderable. They inspire one with awe.
Napolean Hill

Two very important concepts—conscious as opposed to subconscious thought and belief systems are the basis for understanding why my approach works.

Consciousness (Conscious vs. Subconscious)

Very early in the program, the approach influences the subconscious mind through conscious programming. Subconscious and conscious thought are confusing concepts. Consciousness is two-fold; we have a conscious consciousness and a subconscious consciousness. The first represents our everyday and current thoughts. The second, our subconscious, is really the sum-total of all conscious thoughts that the mind has accepted and stored.

<u>Consciousness</u>

Conscious Consciousness	**Subconscious Consciousness**
↓	↓
Current Thoughts)	**(Accepted and Stored Thoughts)**

To complicate this process even further, at times, we feed the subconscious through conscious activity, such as using positive statements to influence the subconscious mind. During other times, the subconscious controls and feeds the conscious with activity, such as tying shoes in a habitual manner. When we are awake, we are always operating in a circular fashion with the subconscious and conscious interacting during every millisecond of the day. When we are asleep, the conscious mind is not at work, and the subconscious controls dreams, bodily activities, and other important functions.

Here is an important question to ask—what would we do if we did not have memory, subconscious thought, and established habits? It would be hard to drive a car because we would have to relearn all the steps every time we began. Storing memory into our subconscious is vital to survival. We need our subconscious habits to operate efficiently. Proper, positive habits make life easier and more enjoyable. The inverse is also true—improper, negative habits eat away and destroy us.

The thoughts we have, whether they are subconscious or conscious, are the highest forms of energy in our bodies, and we are responsible for where and how we direct that energy. All our attitudes about who we are, the ideas we have, the beliefs we hold are located in the subconscious.

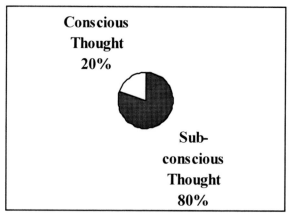

Conscious thought is that which we use during the normal course of our day. We are quite aware of our conscious thoughts because we can easily identify them. Most motivational programs on the market today rely on creating the awareness that influences conscious thought. Think about this—80% of the way we react in our lives comes from subconscious thought. Only 20% of what we do is conscious in nature. Thus, it is easy to see how important it is to try to change the internal, subconscious programs.

Conscious thought when repeated and expressed over and over again becomes subconscious programming and is habitually ingrained, so it is hard to tell whether an expressed thought is coming from the conscious or subconscious thought level. Thoughts cycle continuously, intertwining both conscious and subconscious thoughts. We do not think about what we are doing most of the time. Instead, we react instinctively from our subconscious programming.

Before the subconscious can be altered, an individual has to travel through the entire learning curve, go through all of the stages. Only then is change to the subconscious possible. My approach is designed to transport a person through all of the steps necessary to change.

Belief Systems

Everything we know consists of a belief of some kind which influences our lives—second by second, day by day. When counseling a couple, I start by asking what the problem seems to be in the relationship. After getting both sides of the story, I stop and explain that based on their individual belief systems, each is correct; both viewpoints have merit. Sometimes, this leads to more confrontation and finger pointing. After further explanation about how we have developed our belief systems, we begin to make progress. When we consider that at one time the Earth was believed to be flat and was later discovered to be round, we realize that what we think is true may not be so.

What we believe to be fact is often relative and dependent upon the semantics of the situation. Facts almost always depend upon some of our assumptions and the perspectives we bring to the situation—all of which are beliefs. Our thinking would be much more open and flexible if we considered most *facts* to be *useful beliefs* that we have *made up*.

Examples of Individual Beliefs

During my dating years, I experienced two humorous situations in which the conflict of different belief systems really reared its ugly head. On one occasion, I was having dinner at a restaurant for the first time with a lady who commented to me that one thing she did not like in a man was for him use his finger to help put food on his fork. I don't do that so I just let the comment pass; however, a few minutes later, she asked to excuse herself so she could go outside to smoke a cigarette. We were not even finished eating! I did not comment on how I felt about her request because it was obvious she was hooked on smoking. I do remember thinking, as she left to go smoke, about a comment a friend made to me about dating smokers, "Kissing a smoker is like licking a dirty ash tray." She believed lax table manners were repugnant. I believed smoking was undesirable. Needless to say, that was our first and last date.

Another person I dated corrected me every time I asked for something such as salt, pepper, or butter, by saying "pass me the butter." When I received it, I would thank the person. She wanted me to say, "please pass the butter." In my family of nine people, we grew up using the "pass the butter—thank you" routine and in her family it was "please pass the butter." She became so irritated with me that she would ignore me in public if I did not say it her way while I was eating. I would just sit there with no food until I did it her way. Her belief was that my actions were impolite. My belief was that she was making a mountain out of a mole hill and that her public reactions were rude—two different belief systems in conflict.

How We Learn Our Beliefs

Children seldom misquote us. In fact, they usually repeat every word that we should not have said. They learn from our examples. The following anecdote demonstrates how children learn beliefs from their parents:

A mother invited guests to dinner. At the table she turned to her six-year old daughter and said, "Would you like to say the blessing?"

"I don't know what to say," the girl replied.

"Just say what you have heard Mommy say," the mother stated.

The daughter bowed her head and said, "Lord, why on earth did I invite all these people to dinner?"

Sometimes, we develop false beliefs based on limited information. The following story about six blind men and an elephant provides an appropriate setting for assumptions to be drawn without sufficient data:

Each man touched a part of the elephant to determine what it was. The first man touched the elephant's tusks and decided that it was some type of spear because it was sharp, hard, coarse and sturdy. The second man touched the elephant's tail and concluded that it was some type of rope or whip. The third man thought it was some type of wall since it had a rough texture and was very firm. The fourth man, touching the elephant's trunk, decided that it was some type of animal, probably a snake because it was long, easy to bend, and had a strange texture. The fifth man, touching the ear, thought it was some kind of plant. It felt like a large leaf because of its texture and size. The sixth man touched one of the legs and was convinced that it was a log or branch of a tree. He had already heard from one of the other men that the object felt like a leaf.

They were all wrong. They had only touched a small part of the whole and formed incorrect conclusions based on their belief systems.

Beliefs Systems Are Important!

Our belief systems are very important because we cannot live without them. Therefore, it is vital for you to determine exactly what your beliefs are and which ones are preventing you from becoming the dynamic person you wish to be. If you take the approach that you are always right, you are telling yourself that you do not need to grow. Nevertheless, if you remain open to new ideas and the possibility that your beliefs may be inaccurate, you challenge yourself and continue to improve who you are. It is the individual who believes that he always knows the right answer who has trouble throughout life. Most do not realize that inappropriate belief systems lock them into dead-end lives.

Secondly, your beliefs about yourself are sometimes hard to understand because they come from years of programming that is stored in the subconscious mind. These beliefs are difficult to change. One of the main purposes of this book is to provide an understanding of what it will take to change your beliefs into positive, productive, successful, loving beliefs. How worthy of success in life do you believe yourself to be? Weak ineffectual beliefs about yourself can undermine all that you are trying to become.

As soon as we change or repair beliefs, we change the reality of our lives. When you begin to change, you will be surprised at how open you are to other new ideas. Albert Einstein once said:

> ## The real nature of things,
> ## we shall never know, never.

Consequently, we function best as individuals who learn, grow, and remain flexible to change.

Chapter Six

The Learning Curve

> My Life is one long curve, full of turning points.
> **Pierre Trudeau**

One of the major points of interest I found during the research of my technique was that an actual learning curve exists that everyone experiences during the twenty one-day period. Information about the curve is a great tip off as to how our minds change when using new materials.

If you persist and follow the program for twenty-one days, you will find that the program follows a pattern. The program starts out as either strange or fun for one to three days because it is new and different. Next, a resistance period commences which lasts six to seven days. Although resistance doesn't disappear, a new learning period from seven to fifteen days occurs when you begin memorizing the statements, predicting which one will come next in the program. Lastly, your mind accepts the information.

Learning Curve Time Frame

Days	Reactions
1-3	Strange and Fun Feelings
Positive Feelings	
Subtle and Gradual Changes	
	Word-Activated Learning
1-10	Mind Resistance

New Awareness	
	New Broadcasting
15-21	Personalization of Programs
15-21	Manifestation of Goals
Reliving the Past	
21	Point of Acceptance

Beginning Period (1-3 Days)

During the first few days of the program, participants in my research felt one of two ways: (1) some had fun, enjoying the novelty of the experience; (2) others, however, felt embarrassed or even silly as they talked to themselves in positive ways. Each day, we talk to other people, but we have been taught that talking to ourselves is strange. Actually, psychologists use the approach of having patients talk to themselves in therapy. As several clients stated, "I found talking to myself unnatural." Others noted that they did not identify with their voice, "Who is this stranger?"

Some of the embarrassed individuals had difficulty with the positive statements because they felt they were bragging on themselves. Others felt uncomfortable, believing that people might view them as weird. If this occurs, remember that it is simply an adjustment period experienced by many who have preceded you through program use. Talking to yourself in a positive way is necessary to influence your subconscious mind. Bear in mind, the final outcome you are trying to achieve. Conduct the program in privacy until the awkward period passes and your participation feels more natural.

Positive Feelings (1-21 Days)

A side effect surfaced immediately in the research. Use of the positive programs created improved attitudes and a sense of well-being. In psychology, this is referred to as a situational positive, conscious effect. The positive words were creating a warm feeling, caused by a change in the chemical reactions of the body. Dr. Wayne Dwyer, a noted motivational writer and speaker, said it best:

When you think positive, happy, loving thoughts, there's a different chemistry that goes into your body than when you think depressing, negative, anguishing, and disparaging thoughts.

Jake, one of my clients commented: "Using the tape program is similar to taking a drug. The drug gives you a high, just like the tape program." Of course, an important difference must be noted: use of drugs has dreadful side effects; whereas, the use of my program has positive, lasting effects.

Have you ever tried talking to yourself in a positive manner for fifteen minutes a day? Try it and you will be amazed at the results. Consider this—we are fundamentally mental creatures. You can *think* yourself into being unhappy with negative thoughts and comments. The opposite is true; you can *think* yourself into being happy about your life with positive thoughts and words. Hence, many believe laughter is great medicine. It brings a positive-charged chemistry into the mix. Because my wife believes in laughter so strongly, she has a plaque displayed on a bookcase in our home that reads, "Laughter is the music of the soul."

With positive thoughts and words you can think yourself into being well, into becoming prosperous, into success. When you become the master of your own thinking, your wishes can come true. Remember, you are predominately a thinker. Your slightest thought creates energy, which allows what you have been thinking to enter your reality. People who learn how to control their thinking learn how to control their destinies. The moment we realize that our thoughts have the power to create is the moment we are freed from our subconscious bondage.

We all know that we must exercise and eat properly to maintain a healthy body. Doesn't it make sense to maintain a healthy mind? You should start to exercise your mind by talking to yourself for fifteen minutes a day. These "surprise benefits," a positive attitude and a sense of well-being, are worth the effort. It is a quicker, easier, cheaper, and healthier way of getting high—a natural high.

We are the only living creatures that can change our biology by the way we think and feel. We actually create awareness within ourselves, and this awareness creates a mental state that dictates changes in our body. Every cell in our body is constantly eavesdropping on our thoughts and reacting in the way the thoughts are projected. Negative thoughts can create critical outcomes to our physical being, while optimistic thoughts can strengthen our immune systems.

Positive influences on the cells in the body can speed up or retard the processes of such things as aging, disease, and atrophy. Researchers have publicized cases where illnesses in the body have actually been reversed. The great cyclist, Lance Armstrong, overcame life-threatening, testicular cancer to rebound and win the Tour de France—four times. He and his family strongly believe that his positive determination was an integral part of his recovery. As an individual, you have more control than you ever dreamed over the direction of your life. Just as Lance Armstrong, all you have to do is develop the kind of positive thinking illustrated in his book *It's Not About the Bike*.

You may not realize that words and thoughts shape who you are by triggering intelligence located throughout your cells. For instance, if you think about the taste of a lemon, your mouth may water in response to your concentration. Images and words trigger human responses. Similarly, all you have to do is think positive, loving thoughts about yourself, and you will create an optimistic feeling throughout your body. Participants in my research noticed a remarkable difference when they used positive, personal statements.

Psychological distress is extremely powerful and causes more illness than any other known factor. The beliefs, assumptions, expectations, and self-images that are triggered by our thoughts influence all the biochemistry in our bodies. Changes in our biochemistry further complicate or compound other imbalances throughout the body until we succumb to a state of dysfunction. I had a friend who went through a major storm at sea during which the lives of all aboard the ship were in serious danger. A day after the incident, his hair turned white and has stayed that way ever since. Professional therapists have learned that strong thoughts of fear or grief have the ability to cause both long-term and short-term impacts. Doctors have begun to realize that intensely negative situations may cause any number of physical ailments. One quick and easy way to get back to a more normal state is to think more positively. The reverse happens and the body returns to internal equilibrium.

I was so impressed with the information, showing that positive words create positive feelings, that I produced a tape called "Kick Start Your Day." Many times, negative information coming from our jobs, family, children, or communities create the need for some positive feelings. When we cannot muster positive attitudes due to difficult circumstances, we need to "jump start ourselves." Use this program in the morning before beginning your day or any time that life seems out of control or overwhelming. If you start using the program when depressed, at first, it is hard to be positive. Later, four or five minutes into the program, a change occurs and your attitudes shifts from negative to positive. Four positive statements from twenty different programs are provided so that all areas of your life are covered. Examples from the program include the following:

"I am a positive, caring person;" "My life is very harmonious;" "I am relaxed and calm;" "I live a joyful, fun life;" "I have a zest for life;" "My life is carefree and simple;" "I am a very special person;" "My potential to achieve is unlimited;" "I feel young and exciting."

The program continues with approximately seventy-five, positive statements.

Subtle and Gradual Change (1—21 days)

There are two critical aspects important to gradual change over a twenty-one day period: possessing potential which you have not tapped, and wishing to change.

If you meet both criteria, you will begin to program new positive, supporting information into your subconscious mind. It soon becomes exciting and something upon which you can build. Long-term change occurs once you go through the resistance period, and it takes little effort to continue the process because you realize the long-term benefits.

Most learning is long term. However, there are times when we learn in one exposure—immediately. I mention this because I do not want you to expect the programs to create instant success. As Lois concluded six months later, "The program is so subtle that you do not realize you are changing because it is gradual. One day, I woke up to the fact that my life had actually changed in ways I never thought possible."

Most of what we learn happens over an extended period of time and is, in fact, not very painful. Some of our experiences do occur as a by-product of instant pain, which immediately creates an acute awareness in our long-term memory. An example of instant pain is a child touching a hot stove and burning his hand—this is an instant learning experience and is immediately entered into the subconscious memory. It would be rare for a child to touch a hot stove again. An example of an extended-learning situation is the child who grows up in a negative environment in which she is constantly criticized. She never feels adequate and develops feelings of poor self worth. This programming occurs over a long period of time but is reinforced daily, making the beliefs and behaviors permanent.

To alter a poor self image, individuals must have a variety of positive reinforcement in their lives, offsetting the old behaviors. There are actually two methods of changing this type of behavior. One is repeating a new response over an extended period of time until one day the approach has reprogrammed the person. This is what my technique is all about: positive, consistent programming. The other option is to enter into extensive therapy in which a therapist moves the individual through a series of exploratory discoveries about her/his life. The work must continue until the old behavior is understood and modified to the extent that an improved behavior results. This approach takes a vast amount of time and money.

We understand that learning will occur if we acquaint ourselves with new information and if we are persistent. If the information is contrary to established, subconscious memory, we need, however, to apply the twenty one-day/twenty-one time theory to build new patterns of behavior.

Chapter Seven

The Power of Words (1-21 days)

> Handle them carefully, for words have more power than atomic bombs.
> **Pearl Strachan**

Another major revelation occurred when users in the research study recognized the power of words. The program, built around a central theme with supporting positive statements, helped to create a new awareness. Since between 75-80 percent of what people cope with daily is negative information gathered during early childhood, the subconscious mind is shaped by all of this negativity. As strange as it may seem, most of our useful programming contains a high percentage of negative content, which is counterproductive to us and actually works against us throughout our lives.

Sticks and stones will break my bones, but words will wound me forever.

The above statement is the title to the first chapter of a book by Douglas Block and Jon Merritt called Positive Self-Talk for Children. I recommend the book as a good source to find affirming statements on all kinds of subjects. Block states:

Words are influential for a simple reason—each word or phrase spoken to a child carries with it an underlying message about the child and his relationship to the world. Once the child internalizes this message, it becomes a belief that governs his future experience.

Most of the time we are not conscious of our beliefs because they are programmed subconsciously; nonetheless, they affect us for the rest of our lives. We may have developed a sense of rejection, of not being wanted, or of being unworthy. Such feelings create an unconscious sense of guilt or self-condemnation and give rise, later in life, to what is called an inferiority complex.

Thoughts and Words

When I am teaching a seminar around the concept of thoughts and words, I hold up a pencil and ask, "where did this pencil come from?' Most people will say the store, my office, from a pencil holder, or whatever. In fact, a pencil or anything in life starts with a thought.

Look at a pencil. It looks simple in design doesn't it? Actually, a pencil is not simple. Someone had to think about making lead and encasing it inside a wooden frame. Imagine how complicated it must have been to figure out how to make the thin lead that goes inside a small piece of wood. How does it get inside the pencil? How does the eraser get inserted onto the end of the wooden pencil? How do they paint the pencil the various colors? And on and on! Not as simple as you once thought, is it? Realize that everything that went into making a simple but complex pencil originated within the confines of someone's thought processes.

Words Activate our Intelligence!

At this point, someone in the seminar will ask where a thought comes from—there is always one in each class. I like this question because I can inquire, "First, tell me where is your intelligence located?" Again, the majority of the group will say "in our brains," which is only partially correct.

I draw a circle on the board and ask what they see. Most will say a circle. Right answer, but with a few squiggly marks in the circle (DNA), I can make a cell. The intelligence network in our bodies is located on these DNA strips. Since our bodies are made up of cells—millions and millions of cells with each cell containing its own set of intelligence—the right answer is that our intelligence is located in every cell in our body, including the cells in our brain. Our bodies are guided by DNA intelligence and our physiology is nothing but intelligence at work. Every process underway in our bodies is intelligence talking to itself.

Because our intelligence is abstract and invisible, it has to react before it is made visible to the world. We can say our body makes its intelligence known by the molecules that carry messages. There is actually very little difference between a molecular reaction and the thoughts which we express through words. Our intelligence reacts to the words and concepts that we have learned during our lives.

Talking to your intelligence is a wonderful exercise. How does this happen? If you realize that your intelligence is located on the DNA found in every cell of your body, you know that when you activate that intelligence, you can create what you want. I like to envision a "tiny little person" located in each cell with the primary job of carrying out the intelligence located on the DNA. What becomes important is how to get this person to carry out a function.

Normally, the cell simply activates itself depending on its purpose. Cells exist for different reasons in the heart, lungs, liver, or any part of the body. They also react to what is going on in our lives. If we are stressed, they send out chemicals to handle the stress. If we are happy, they send out chemicals to cope with happiness.

Cause and Effect

What happens with continued use of a program? Your body converts your thoughts, wishes, and desires from the abstract to the concrete. If you hear the words, "I love myself," a warm glow begins to flow through you. This emotion has transformed the molecules of your cells, creating adrenaline rushes in your bloodstream. More importantly, your body feels transformed, the world appears less frightening, and everyday problems seem to vanish. When you think such words as peace, love, or harmony, you become peaceful and loving and experience harmony.

How did the body ever learn about such words as love or hate and right or wrong? It all started with the language we use to refer to ourselves and with early programming from parents, grandparents, aunts, uncle, teachers, siblings, and acquaintances. In his book Ageless Body, Timeless Mind, Dr. Deepak Chopra explains:

> By implication, the language we use to refer to ourselves is of tremendous importance. Child psychologists have found that young children are much more deeply influenced by negative statements from their parents (e.g., "You're a bad boy;" "You're a liar;" "You're not as smart as your sister.") than by prescriptive statements (e.g., "Always wash your hands before eating;" "Don't put your toys in your mouth.") In other words, telling a child what he is makes a much deeper impression than telling him what to do. The mind-body system actually organizes itself around such verbal experiences, and the wounds delivered in words can create far more permanent effects than physical trauma. We literally create ourselves out of words.

Words are Powerful!

How powerful are words? If we change the words we use, can we change our reality? Words help you alter your perception of life and when that happens, you begin to change your world. Every stressful reaction buried deep in your subconscious mind and forgotten long ago still sends out signals, making you tense, anxious, depressed, doubtful of your abilities, or fearful of success (even though you want success). They are all a part of you and control what you do and become. Douglas Block maintains:

> If words can wound, they can also heal. If words can tear down and destroy, they can also build up and encourage you as well. Instead of being told, "One day you'll be behind bars," what if you were told "you're a winner," "keep up the good work," "you're a bright kid," and "you can do it."

Your interpretation of both the physical and mental world is critical to who you become. You can change the "world of your mind" and your body by simply changing your perception. Your cells hold imprints of your beliefs containing maps of your past sufferings or joyous experiences.

Do you want these old imprints to be positive or negative? You have the opportunity to alter them to fit a more desired life style.

All of the trillions of our cells are connected and the well being of our total system is modified when we create a positive, loving world. The positive, inner feelings and the mind growth that occurs profoundly influence our exterior environments. We will actually begin to re-shape how others view us. Thus, mirroring begins. Others mirror back to us what we are broadcasting or delivering to them.

Conscious awareness is being created every time you use a positive, affirming program. The conscious world of your mind is the directing force of your life. Without a conscious effort to change your world, the subconscious part of who you are will remain the same. Instead of letting the automatic pilot (subconscious thought, beliefs, and habits) rule your world, change your reality by using conscious awareness to create a new you.

Mind and Body Connection

The technique of using value constructs (positive statements) to change the voluntary functions of your life can be used to your advantage. The energy and information within your body become the vehicles, controlled by you, to change the perceptual realities of your world. Suddenly, you wake up one day and find that consistent use has changed the patterns of the past. Your world has changed!

Harmonious interaction begins to occur and extend from the body into the environment in which you live. This may come in many forms, but simply put, if we are sending out negative impulses, we are creating the negative. We destroy the environment, create confrontations with people, or kill each other, much like the small children in our elementary schools or the students in Columbine High School. It is important to produce a healthy, positive consciousness so we can live in a healthy, loving environment.

Chapter Eight

Mind Resistance as an Important Factor (1-10 days)

> Resistance is thought transformed into feeling. Change the thought that creates the resistance, and there is no more resistance.
> **Robert Conklin**

The discovery of mind resistance as an important learning factor emerged from the research. At first, all the participants said the program was fun and exciting or they felt a little strange and awkward. Soon, resistance began to appear. This phenomenon occurred when the ideas introduced into the subconscious were in conflict with established beliefs.

Mind resistance will occur anytime you embark on a new path. The importance of understanding mind resistance cannot be overemphasized. If you attempt to change a simple habit such as opening the door with your left hand (if you are right-handed) for twenty-one days, the effort may cause you to become sick at your stomach. Our minds are programmed for consistency with learned habits. Rightfully so! Without ingrained habits, we would have to relearn everything over and over again—something as simple as riding a bike or eating with utensils. Habits are definitely necessary. It's our negative habits that we would all like to change.

Visualize yourself as a microscopic character in your mind, trying to get your subconscious to accept an idea. You find that a guard, monitoring the gate, is not allowing any new information to enter. "Sorry," the guard states, "we cannot have new material stored here that is not compatible to existing information." Subsequently, you find that new ideas are initially turned away. Even so, if you persist, tenaciously presenting the new data, day in and day out, eventually it will be accepted. After wearing down the guard, the gate will open. Such perseverance requires a lot of repetition.

The constant repetition—or the twenty-one-day theory—prevents the mind from creating permanent resistance patterns. The guard, having heard the new idea repeatedly, begins to declare, "I have heard that information before. It is okay to enter; I'll accept the information."

Natural Phenomenon

After the first two or three days of using the program, all kinds of excuses surface in an attempt to stop your efforts. Your mind will say such things as "I know these words; this is too simple; I do not need to continue; this is a waste of my time; I can do without this material; I am not sure this will work; this is too idealistic; nothing else has worked, why should this work; this is silly;" and on and on.

For several research participants, mind resistance appeared immediately. Research indicated strong resistance, especially when individuals used the forgiveness program. Most people associate forgiveness with approval, and they feel conflicted between their desire to forgive and their belief that they have been wronged. We want to forgive people in our lives but forgiveness does not require acceptance. We can forgive someone without condoning his actions or continuing contact. Forgiveness means letting go of bitterness and revengefulness. It does not mean that you need to maintain a friendship with the individual.

Even though thoughts, such as revenge and bitterness, may be negative and counterproductive, many people find themselves comfortable with them. After all, persons can only be who they are and can only know what they know. It is unreasonable to expect people to know more than they know. I often explain to people who reject new opinions, "You only know what you know you know."

Ignorance and closed-minds cause humans to continuously "reinvent the wheel. Many individuals, even the most educated, have to learn from experience even when they have all the answers to the problem before them. Stock traders are a good example. All the successful stock traders about whom I have read claim that they unnecessarily lost thousands of dollars in the beginning of their careers even though there are numerous books on the subject. Even after reading them, the traders refused to follow the "rules" until they had learned from costly mistakes. A friend who is a clinical psychologist explained to me that after years of counseling divorced couples, he did not realize the emotional pain involved in a divorce until he went through his own.

It almost seems as if we have to experience things personally before learning that our subconscious minds cannot recognize and assimilate information if it does not correspond to what is already known. Mind resistance is real, and the experiences of the people who used the programs highlighted the significance of paying attention to why we do not change, even when presented with valuable information that will help us change.

Aerobics of the Mind

Using my programs is similar to attending a mental aerobic class. Often, we begin an exercise program, buy expensive equipment, or join health clubs, only to let the resistance factors stop our exercising. However, if we force ourselves to continue fitness programs for twenty-one successive days and overcome the resistance, we begin to feel better and desire the exercise. Gradually, we have incorporated the exercise regimen into our lives without realizing when or why it happened.

Look at all the weight loss programs on the market today. How many have been tried? Still, Americans are extremely overweight. We fail because we have become subconsciously programmed to eat more than we need. "Have you tried the grande chalupa," or drunk the "super soda?" "Did somebody say juicy hamburger?" Of course, we are all conditioned by advertising propaganda without realizing it. It is hard to watch television without seeing the same ad over and over. The situation is not without hope. We have the power to begin reprogramming our minds. If an individual wants healthy drinks, he should enjoy eight glasses of water each day for twenty-one days, and he will have formed a new habit.

One important idea should be noted. With my programs, you can easily begin reprogramming your mind. Using positive statements is not as expensive as buying exercise equipment or trying a new weight-loss program. They are inexpensive and easy to use. Most of all, possessing a positive attitude is a healthy way to live. Isn't it time to get acquainted with the "guardian of your gate?"

Two Forms of Resistance

Two forms of resistance occur in relation to my programs. The first type emerges when you introduce a statement in the present tense (example: I have unlimited financial resources.), yet the statement is not a current reality. Other examples may be your stating that you have a wonderful relationship with your spouse when, in fact, you do not, or that you are a forgiving person and your mind says, "Whoa, wait a minute. Are you sure you are really forgiving; remember just the other day you would not forgive your neighbor?" This concept is covered in more detail later in the book.

The second resistance form is not as obvious because we have no idea what is actually stored in the subconscious. At first, the mind tries the subtle, soft approach. This type of resistance I found interesting. A client named Bobbi, upon beginning a program, immediately made the statement, "I already know the words." Of course, she knew the words but her belief system did not feel and accept the positive statements as being true. She recognized the words but was unable to believe the concept. She did not love herself. For example, when you hear the statements, "I love myself; I have excellent health; I am a kind and loving person;" you will know and understand all of these words. However, do you truly love yourself; are you in excellent health; are you a kind and loving person? Knowing the words does not make anything so. It is what you believe that is important. That is why I have developed twenty-one days of repetition around a central theme. The hypothesis is that we will reach deep into the recesses of the subconscious mind, alter the negative agenda, and exchange it for positive programming.

Have you read a book and suddenly noticed after reading a whole page, you did not understand what you had read? You had read the words but had not comprehended the meaning. We seek subconscious, not conscious programming. Knowing the words is a conscious process, but repetition of the words must occur before we can make an impression on the subconscious mind. When acceptance occurs, the words, "I love myself; I have excellent health; I am a kind and loving person;" will have a deeper, more valuable meaning in our belief system. Don't fall for resistance-oriented messages such as:

"I have heard that enough; I know it now."

"This is so simple I can learn it in one or two days and save a lot of time."

"I know this will not change me."

"This tape program is foolish and I am going to stop."
"This is a total waste of my time and money."

Much like dieting, persons often break down and start thinking negatively again. They think that one piece of cake or one extra helping of potatoes will not interfere with their mission to lose weight. Individuals wanting to break an addictive habit may think that one drink will not hurt them. They smoke a joint or snort cocaine just to show their self control. Their minds tell them that once will not hurt them.

Expect your mind to try all types of tricks—guilt, fear, doubt, unworthiness, discouragement, or anger—to stop you from achieving what you set out to accomplish. Give yourself credit. You have much more power to manipulate yourself than you realize. When the mind is in resistance, it becomes very creative during the struggle to change. As Ernest Holmes mentions in his book, <u>This Thing Called Life</u>:

> **One thing is certain, our subject or unconscious (subconscious) thought patterns can be changed. We have created them and we can change them.**

That's right—you, not the recorded series, are the source of resistance. Always remember the difference between conscious and subconscious thought. Do not be fooled by the fact that your subconscious thought is prodding your conscious mind to react in the way the subconscious wants.

Chapter Nine

New Broadcasting (15-21 Days)

> Whenever you are Thinking something,
> you are Broadcasting it in a subtle way
> **Osho**

Persons in the research study began to notice how they had changed the way they talked to others, using the words and phrases learned from the recordings. The new programming was starting to become a part of their reality. The old, negative programs were being reformatted with the use of new, positive value constructs, adding a more optimistic force to their lives. Users found that they would say such things as, "You really look great today;" "I find what you are saying to be extremely valuable;" or "You're such a kind, caring person." Sometimes, they used even more interesting comments like, "You look happier." This is referred to as a triggering situation when personal programs "I feel great today" suddenly become "You really look great today." Since we are a mental broadcasting station, what we put out to others comes back to us exactly in the same manner. I discuss triggering in a later chapter.

My daughter Katie shocked me one day while I was driving. She said, "Dad!"

"Yes, Katie."

"I love myself; I am a kind, gentle, loving person. I am awesome."

It took me a second to realize what was going on and then I replied, "Katie, you have been listening to your dad's tapes, haven't you?"

"Yes, Dad," she replied, "I listen to them every night before I go to bed."

Her listening to my tapes isn't the miracle of the story. Katie was born in distress and suffered neurological damage. She could not speak until she was seven. I remember sitting with her on the sofa when she was three and working with her for hours on her sounds. She could make all kinds of animal sounds, a tiger being her favorite, but she could not say words. We enrolled her in a signing class and she communicated by sign language until age seven. At age seven, her cognitive development started maturing and she began to talk. I will always remember her first experience with speech.

Katie had special needs and other children did not want to spend much time with her. She had a lazy eye, walked funny, and could not speak. When she was tested at age three, we were told that she was a borderline, mentally retarded child. I never bought into her test results because I was too aware of the excellent recall that she possessed. Today, Katie has a normal life. She is in the eleventh grade, doing well in school, and employed in a part-time job. So you see, when Katie told me, "Dad I love myself; I am a kind, gentle, loving person. I am awesome," it meant the world to me. Even today, Katie has a very healthy self-concept. I know the self-esteem tape that she listened to contributed greatly to this feeling. Recall the phrase, "you are what you think you are, maybe more but never less." Katie likes herself, perhaps more than she realizes.

Furthermore, Katie made the switch from negative to positive. She had successfully replaced a negative attitude with a positive one. Instead of thinking she was inferior to other children, she had developed an appreciation for who she was—a kind and gentle person who loved herself just as she had told me. Of course, her father has always believed that she is "awesome."

It was apparent during research that the programs were beginning to alter the subconscious mind. Users were internalizing the materials and beginning to apply them to their daily lives. This permanent change of the belief system was a major breakthrough and one of the critical things for which I was searching. The programs had created a new database—a positive foundation extremely helpful in changing all aspects of who we are.

Concentration and Meaning (15-21 Days)

Almost everyone using the tapes in the research study expressed that they had experienced a new awareness sometime after the thirteenth day. They found themselves spending more time concentrating to comprehend what the statements meant. In other words, the individuals began to believe that what they were saying could actually happen. The routine became fun, exciting, and even realistic. At this point, three factors are operating—(1) the mind begins to acknowledge the statement, (2) the acknowledgement allows the statements to acquire more importance, and (3) new feelings and attitudes develop. Shortly thereafter users realized they had begun to expound or elaborate on the statements.

Create your own Program (15-21 days)

When I first developed the programs, one option I considered was to help each person create her/his own, individualized tapes. I soon realized that this was impractical because of the time and expense it would take to assist each person. I needed something more generic, so with the advice of friends, I decided to develop programs centered around one central theme—concepts that we felt would benefit larger numbers.

When individuals reached the fifteen through eighteen-day period, they learned the statements and knew which one was coming next. It was at this point that a user began to elaborate or make the statement more personal. Strong personal feelings about the statements resulted. Here are examples of how the statements changed:

Statement	Potential Changes Made to Statement
I love myself.	Today more than ever, I really love myself.
I have a lot of confidence	I am the most confident person I have ever met.
I like myself	I like, love, and accept who I am; I'm incredible.

I am an excellent golfer.	I am a cool, confident, awesome golfer.
I am an excellent learner.	I learn easily; I'm smart and do excellent work.
I am a powerful person.	I (your name) am so powerful it amazes me!
I am in control of myself.	I am in control and love myself and my life!
Life is exciting and energizing.	I am excited and totally energized this morning.
I am a caring person.	I am not only a caring person but also extremely loving and nurturing.
I am a healthy person.	I (your name) am healthy, vivacious, and love my life today.

You cannot feel or hear the inflections or intonations as you read the above statements, but during this period of learning, a person's energy level increases.

It is this new learning phase that allows users both the freedom and power to take the statements and make them their own. You will find yourself singing, shouting, whispering, or even acting comically to say the statements in different ways. You are talking to your mind, using positive, affirming statements in a loving, dramatic, or creative way. This was one of the biggest surprises—the opportunity to take the simple statements from any of the tapes and build personalized programs.

Chapter Ten

Manifesting Occurs (15-21 Days)

Our subconscious minds have no sense of humor, play no jokes and cannot tell the difference between reality and an imagined thought or image. What we continually think about eventually will manifest in our lives.
Robert Collier

I was selling tapes to a group to whom I had presented a seminar when one member asked me an extremely important question. She wanted to know how the program helped me. I had to go home that night to think and write down what had happened to me since I first started using the tapes. The next morning, I was able to outline to her in detail how my life had improved. She immediately bought one of the tape series. The programs do not create instant change except for the feeling of wellness. The long-range effects occur as a byproduct of living your life. In my life, I've enjoyed more inner peace, less conflict with others, more prosperity, and better health, as well as a fabulous relationship with my wife, three wonderful children, and personal happiness, joy and harmony. All of this happened because I was changing my thinking habits from negative to positive.

To think is to create. Ask yourself—am I a thinker? Do I think before I react? If you believe you are a thinker, and you should, you are therefore a creator of your life. Consequently, you live in a world of your own creation. If all you do is react, you live in a world where life happens to you. You may not have managed your world when you were young, but as a teenager or adult, you should begin to control your world, not let the world control you.

Often, I tell my students this important phrase, "You have the power in each and every millisecond of the day to change who you are—you make the decisions that can change your life forever." At first, you may deny it, believing you are trapped in the life to which you were born. Nonetheless, with the assistance of my programs, you will come to see that this is true. If this were not true, you would not be a "free" individual. If it is true, you are "free" to modify your life. Think about it—this is an impressive capacity you possess. Change what you are thinking, and indeed, you change your world because your thoughts become manifested into your life. Wayne Dyer's book <u>Manifest Your Destiny</u> illustrates how people have the potential to influence their futures.

The end product of any good program will be the actualization of your desires. When this happens, the objective has been manifested into your life. It was a few years after I discovered the programs that the actual reason for personal verbalization of the statements became clear to me. It came like a bolt of lightning that the use of one's voice has much more personal significance. Your voice commands you directly to do what is necessary to achieve your goals. It is similar to what Jesus stated centuries ago—"Ask and you shall receive."

Many things you manifest take years to achieve. If you want to be an architect and ask to become one, you may develop a positive, affirming program to convince your mind that you have the talent and commitment to become an architect. What happens next? Well, a lot has to happen, from enrollment in college to the completion of a degree and certification. It will all happen—just not immediately. The end result will be that you have manifested the fortitude to become an architect.

Believe! Believe! Believe!

There is one key requirement you must have to make all of this work—making yourself believe it will happen. In other words, you must banish the doubt that it is possible. Strange isn't it? You must convince yourself that you can achieve what you want, that you are the *key* to your success or failure in life. By progressing far enough along the learning curve, you are able to convince your subconscious mind that what you are saying is true.

Suddenly, the mind begins to believe that it is true. And what happens next? You start to create what you want—what you are manifesting.

As a student, I often heard the phrase, "As you think, so shall you be." I also heard, "What you think about expands." If you have negative thoughts, you expand those negative thoughts. Anything you can imagine in your mind is possible.

In the beginning, we have trouble accepting that we have the ability to manifest what we want, simply by concentrating on what we want, but as the old adage says, "God helps those who help themselves." We have to banish any doubt that we can get what we desire. We must be willing to receive what we want and do what is necessary to achieve results. Positive, affirming statements are a way of tricking the mind into believing that we already have what we want. The statements are in the present tense—"I have; I am." Continuous use eventually convinces the mind to believe it can happen, so we do what is necessary to achieve what we have been manifesting or affirming.

Take a Boat Trip!

Visualize your life similar to a journey on a speed boat. As you sit in the stern of the boat, I want you to answer three questions, but first, look into the water and see the wake created by the movement of the boat.

> Question 1: What is the wake? (The wake is the trail left behind caused by the movement of the boat.)
> Question 2: What is driving the boat? (It is being driven by the energy created by an engine.)
> Question 3: Is it possible for the wake to drive the boat? (No, the wake is the trail left behind and it cannot move the boat.)

Our lives work in similar ways. Our past is like the wake and cannot drive the boat; however, we often wish to blame the past for our present situations. The only thing that has the power and energy to drive the boat is the engine, just as we are the only force that can propel our lives. It is time to quiet the mind chatter from the past because it will not help manifest our desires for the future. The past is the past—gone and powerless, for as the poet Henry Wadsworth Longfellow so eloquently describes:

Look not mournfully into the past. It comes not back again. Wisely improve the present. It is thine. Go forth to meet the shadowy future, without fear.

The past should not drive the ship of your life, so work diligently on letting it go. (In a few paragraphs, I will explain how this can happen.) Only your existing energy can get you what you are trying to manifest. As soon as you are orientated to the present moment, you will create a new reality for yourself.

Creating the Future!

My son asked me one day about prosperity and my prosperity tape. He wanted to know if a homeless person, standing on a street corner begging for food, could listen to my tape and bring prosperity into his/her life. The answer is simple—yes, it could happen, as long as the person did not suffer from substance addiction or mental illness. At first, the homeless person would not believe it possible, but if he listened to the tapes long enough, he would begin to think more optimistically and begin acting in a manner that would draw more prosperity into his life. The reason is clear. As we think, so shall we be. We must be careful about what we think. All of our thoughts, including our doubts, will manifest into our lives. The danger comes if we continually have doubts because we will offset the good we are trying to produce. If we have doubts about ceasing to smoke, we sabotage opportunities to be tobacco free.

Reliving the Past (18-21 Days)

During the last eighteen to twenty-one days in the research, not all, but many people expressed the occurrence of a strange phenomenon. They were beginning to recall past, negative experiences, yet this time, the memories were not threatening. After the events resurfaced, individuals were better able to cope with what had happened. None of the users expressed any anxiety surrounding the remembrances, only relief that they no longer felt the pain of old wounds.

Often, we suppress our past sufferings. For some, this is an opportunity to revisit memories and begin to feel differently. For others who dwell on the past, the experience is a way of releasing old hurts. In almost every case, people in the research study expressed a newfound sense of peace and contentment. They finally felt freedom from the past. I was not sure what brought about this surprise benefit and preferred to call it a benefit because the outcome was helpful. What had transpired allowed new positive thoughts heal the negative wounds of the past. The new beliefs canceled out the older, less productive ones and triggered the mind to release the past wounds for healing. The "guardian of the gate" to the mind had permitted the new, positive programming to supersede the old negative thoughts.

If past hurts surface, you should not be alarmed, rather view the experience as a natural consequence of using the programs. Continued use of the program will help build more positive feelings about the past and eventually neutralize the pain.

Chapter Eleven

Designing Your Program

Simple things should be simple and complex things should be possible.
Alan Kay

Step One—Three Choices

"Secret ingredient" number one is all about how the program is orchestrated. You have three choices before proceeding further.

- The first choice is to look ahead at all the programs in Appendix B. Here, you will find actual programs to use, or you can take statements from the programs to build your own program.
- Your second choice is to use the material in the book to learn how to build your own program.
- The third choice is to purchase a program already designed and recorded. Email us at **mediapmf@gmail.com** for information about already designed programs.

I learned from the *Voice* that there are actually three different types of positive statements that exist and not just one positive statement we normally call affirmations. I explain in detail in the next three chapters how to use them in the proper format. The value constructs include affirmations, positive affirming statements, and instructive positive statements. Each develops differently through thought, word and action, strengthening the concept that you are trying to develop.

Basically, value constructs are used to develop a pathway to our subconscious mind. After acceptance, the statements act as triggering devices, producing improved feelings and attitudes in daily life. There is nothing magical about positive statements and they work when used properly. Whatever we affirm will happen, especially as we begin to view it as truth. We benefit from the eventual outcome even though it may take time, patience, and repetition of the concepts. The transformation occurs because a positive statement neutralizes a negative one.

Step Two—Your Own Personal Statements

I agree with many authors who believe that saying mindless affirmations over and over again does little to create new pathways within the brain. Martin Seligman made such a statement in his book <u>Learned Optimism,</u> "We have found over the years that positive statements you make to yourself have little if any effect with the program formats recommended." I once attended a class on prosperity that asked that we repeat the statement "I am prosperous" one hundred times in the morning and one hundred times in the evening. Because prosperity has a different meaning for each of us, repeating the simple statement, "I am prosperous," was an effort in futility. For instance, when I gave a neighbor a prosperity program, she claimed that she did not want to make a lot of money. I explained to her that prosperity could mean many things, such as finding a more prosperous occupation or just having enough money to live comfortably. Simply stating the same affirmation over and over with little knowledge of the meaning does nothing to change attitudes.

Dr. Shad Helmstetter in his book <u>What to Say When You Talk to Yourself</u> believes in the power of positive thinking, asserting that the concept is "one of the better ideas to come out of self-help literature." He recognizes, however, that making a decision to think positively will not work indefinitely because "the mental program which was already set up in our subconscious mind is the old kind of programming." Helmstetter clarifies:

> **Positive thinking could work, can work, if the negative thoughts we are told to avoid are immediately replaced with the opposite.**

The next three chapters will help you understand how to develop a program around your particular central theme and let you substitute negative thoughts for positive ones. First, you should decide the central theme you want to develop (examples: self-acceptance, a better game of golf, confidence, improvement in sales, or any area of your life that you wish to alter.) Secondly, write down the negative conditions or thoughts around the theme. At this point, you are ready to compose some opposing statements. The thirty-five different programs offered will be of assistance if you wish to refer to them. Look through the programs and pick a statement contradicting your negative feelings. In essence, you are trying to swap old thoughts for new, more positive ones. By applying the basic principles you have learned, you can, with the power of your affirming words, create an opposite force that counteracts or cancels a negative condition.

Chapter Twelve

Statement Development

> Positive thinking affirming statements have the power to silence your negative thoughts and put you in a positive frame of mind.
> **Dr. Harlan Fisher**

First Type—Affirmation Statements

Most motivational speakers talk about affirmations. To affirm anything is to assert that it is so, even when it is not even true. Affirming something is the first step toward creating a desire, which in turn, motivates us to attain whatever it is we are asserting. Through my studies, I have found that many people do not know how to write proper affirmation statements and actually through the writing, violate the original concept and purpose.

What exactly is an affirmation? There are seven things that should be in all affirmation statements. If they do not contain all seven, I consider the affirmation a positive statement or use it as an instructive statement. All three types of statements are necessary to foster the type of programs I recommend.

Important Characteristics of Affirmations:

1. A positive statement asserting a desire to become a certain way, "I am a kind, gentle and loving person."

People often use negative words to try and create a positive outcome. If a smoker states, "Today, I am going to quit smoking," the mind will accept the word smoking but will reject the statement, "Today, I am going to quit." The mind does not want to stop and because it is hearing the word smoking, will actually want to smoke. The subconscious habit to smoke is being reinforced. The mind simply sees the "Today, I am going to . . ." and the person smokes instead of stopping. Developing the Tobacco Free program was difficult because any words that related to smoking or tobacco could not be used. When you do not want something in your life, you need to stop using the words that support that condition. You should not use statements such as, "I will have only six cigarettes today." You will find that immediately after making that statement, you crave a cigarette.

Even words such as "eat" that are used in a weight reduction program have to be carefully written into a program. "I like to eat healthy foods" may cause an individual to eat more. Obviously, the person likes to eat and "eat" is a word that the mind associates with food. The mind accepts "eat" more readily than the words "healthy foods." When developing a program around a negative concept, the individual must eliminate negative words. A better statement would be "I like healthy foods."

2. A personal statement, "I am a confident person."

The statements should always be statements that you affirm for yourself. After all, you wish to change *your* way of thinking, *your* self-image and *your* belief system. Almost all the time your affirmations will be an "I" or "I am" statement. An even more preferable scenario is to use your name in the statement. When saying, "I am a prosperous person," change "I" to your name. "I am" is considered one of the most forceful statements, so you should begin using it.

3. A simple, direct statement, "I am enthusiastic and energetic."

The statements should be short (six to eight words) and no longer than one sentence, yet be flexible with this rule. After you have used a statement once, you may elaborate on it. For example, "I am a loving person" may later be expanded to "I am considered by others to be a kind, gentle, loving person."

You should avoid putting too many topics into one statement. The statements should be direct. You are trying to trigger a concept. When the statements become too long, the mind loses the point of reference. The idea is analogous to the attention-span concept; anything over eighteen minutes makes learning difficult because our mind wanders.

4. Statements with action or state of being words, "I <u>choose</u> to be happy." (action). "I <u>am</u> cheerful." (state of being)

The statements above show action (I choose) or state of being (I am) and are a convincing way of acting as if you already have a specific quality.

5. Use of present tense, "I <u>enjoy</u> interacting well with others."

By using the present tense, you are convincing the conscious and subconscious mind that you already have what you are trying to affirm. "I want success" is a weak affirmation. "I have success" is the proper way to word the statement. "I have" convinces your mind that your success is acceptable. The mind may have trouble comprehending the statement and resistance may develop. The mind believes that it is a lie. If you have difficulty with this kind of directness, alter your statements to sound as if success is imminent or that all things you do will lead to success. I personally like the direct approach, writing direct manifestations as if I already have what I am seeking.

We are talking to ourselves as if we already have what we are asking for and the mind does not know how to handle this data. At this point, mind resistance really begins to be restrictive, but eventually, after hearing the statement over and over again, the mind acts as if it has what it is being told. It begins to move to new desires and motivations. Awareness has been created using the affirmation statement.

6. Use of emotional words, "I <u>love</u> healthy food."

The statements should contain highly charged words that spark an emotional response. Any time you wish to impact on another person, paint an emotional picture. Emotional pictures attract peoples' immediate attention. The same holds true with the writing of affirmations—the more emotionally charged the words, the more they will influence the mind.

7. Use of realistic words.

Make your affirmations realistic. If you want a certain outcome, be pragmatic. One of my clients wrote his statements seeking a salary of one million dollars, so there would be no limitations. I explained that he needed to be reasonable, based on his education and experience. We decided that sixty thousand dollars was more realistic. When you attain the first goal, you can simply raise the amount. Another client desired an ideal person to date. He reported back a week later about five possibilities but none were what he really wanted. I helped him write more definitive and practical statements that would affirm exactly what he desired.

Common Mistakes when Writing Affirmations:

1. "I am getting better and will not let fear trap me." (Never use negative words such as fear or trap—the mind will only hear the words "fear and trap," not the words "getting better.")
2. "Mankind should find love instead of fault." ("Fault" is a negative word and the statement is not personal.)
3. "Death need not be scary." (The mind will hear "death" and "scary." Also, the statement is not personal.)
4. "I will face my pain and not deny it." (The statement is not positive and is in the future, not present tense.)
5. "I will never give up hope." (Never is a good word to use, but the mind may hear "give up hope." Also, the statement is in future tense.)
6. "By not condemning myself today, I always find peace." ("Condemning" is a negative word and the statement is not direct.)
7. "I will not hold grievances against my children." (If you have grievances against your children, the mind will hear that part of the statement.)
8. "I may choose to teach love or to teach fear." ("Teach fear" is negative and "may choose," allows for options.)
9. "I will remember that my mind controls my body and not vice versa." (The statement is not clear or direct.)

10. "I choose to heal my relationship by letting go of my self-condemnation." (The statement is too long and negative in nature—"self-condemnation.")

Affirmations should have the elements of a personal command. You are declaring what you want through verbal directives so you will create what you wish. You should repeat thoughts or use words over and over again—not once, not twice, but many times until your mind accepts and believes what it has been told. The elimination of your doubt about what is being said is the beginning of acceptance, which is the first step toward creating the reality you seek.

Chapter Thirteen

Statement Development—Types Two and Three

> Phrases for self affirming statements can bring about positive changes as desired when they are repeated with conviction.
> **Dr. Harlan Fisher**

Second Type—Positive Statements

The second and probably the most important declaration used is a statement that comes short of being an affirmation but is a strong positive, value construct. It contains most, but not all, of the elements of an affirmation, making it different but vital to the development a total program. Some comparisons include:

"I am an excellent golfer." (affirmation)
"I am becoming a great golfer." (positive statement).

I am an excellent golfer implies that you are already an excellent golfer even though you may not be. I am "becoming" a great golfer implies that you are working to become a terrific golfer. This statement does not fit the affirmation requirement because it lacks the present tense, confirming that you are already an excellent golfer. I like using the positive, affirming statement because it allows for quicker acceptance in the mind and helps to overcome resistance. When using positive, affirming statements, however, I always use supporting affirmations. Incorporating both types in a program is essential.

Sponsoring Words and Thoughts

One of the purposes behind building a solid, positive-thought program is to change sponsoring beliefs and assemble new positive thoughts. Sponsoring thoughts are root thoughts or basic thoughts upon which all others build. A sponsoring thought may be an affirmation but most of the time it is a positive, affirming statement. The following mathematical example will help explain sponsoring thought:

We have a framework based on the principle of ten. Everything in math is built on ten (10 X 1 = 10) (10 X 2 = 20) (10 X 10 = 100). We can build anything in mathematics because we always know the basic sponsoring framework of 10.

It is more difficult to establish the right sponsoring framework in personal ethics or interpersonal relations. By using positive, affirming statements in any form around a core subject, we are assured of building the framework upon which we can later draw. "I am a great golfer" is an example of a sponsoring thought. If a person believes the statement, everything that relates to the idea will be accepted by the mind, like "I have an excellent putting technique." Such basic programming allows you to draw on a sponsoring thought that is both positive in nature and a foundation for growth.

Another example relates to money. Many of us have contradictory attitudes about money: "It is the root of all evil;" "Money doesn't grow on trees;" "Money corrupts;" "People with a lot of money are unhappy." All of these thoughts interfere with the wishes of people who want to earn more money. They do everything possible to sabotage getting money because their root (sponsoring) thought is negative. Changing sponsoring thoughts about money is necessary before individuals can improve their financial situation.

Present experiences are based on previous thoughts. Every thought we have leads to experience, which leads to further thoughts, which in turn leads to further experience. Remember the statement I made in an earlier chapter—"You can only know what you know you know." Our thoughts and experiences revolve in a vicious cycle and we always find ourselves back where we started. Our foundation thoughts do not allow us to expand beyond what we already know.

Triggering Devices

Sponsoring statements become the triggering devices that later release feelings and actions. To understand triggering devices, examine the following advertising slogans developed to manipulate us into buying products:

The Breakfast of Champions!—Wheaties
Do the Dew!—Mountain Dew.
You deserve a break today.—McDonalds.
Winston cigarettes taste good like cigarettes should.
How do you spell relief?—Rolaids.

When we go to the store, seeing the product triggers the slogan etched in our memory, so we purchase the merchandise. To counter such propaganda, if your mind is programmed to drink too many sodas, substitute new triggering devices which promote the drinking of water instead of soft drinks:

I drink eight glasses of water per day.
Water is cool, refreshing and energizing.
Water is free and healthy for me.
Water is wholesome and beneficial for me.

The positive statements help to establish a new, desired belief system. When the belief systems we hold are strengthened, the new triggering statements start to contribute to our overall health. By healing our erroneous thoughts, we actually heal our bodies. By changing our subconscious minds, we change our lives.

Norman Cousin's book, <u>Anatomy of an Illness</u>, describes how he was diagnosed with a terminal illness. After contemplating his life, Cousins realized he seldom laughed or felt joy. He collected all the comedy films he could find, locked himself in a hotel room, and after experiencing hours of humor and laughter, healed his spirit. By dwelling on the positive instead of the negative elements of life, he was able to heal his physical health, as well.

Third Type—Instructive Statements

An instructive statement does not contain all the elements of an affirmation although it is positive in nature but is used as a guide to provide information to the subconscious.

"I am an excellent golfer." (affirmation)
"I am becoming an excellent golfer." (positive affirming statement)
"I pay close attention to my golf grip." (instructive statement)

All three types of statements are necessary to develop a comprehensive program. Nevertheless, when the user wants to instill a process into the mind, the instructive statement is the type to use. Educators profit from the third approach. The following is an example:

1. I know my ABC's (space for saying—I know my ABC's)
2. ABCD (space for saying—ABCD)
3. EFG(space for saying—EFG)
4. HIJK(space for saying-HIJK)
5. LMNOP(space for saying LMNOP)
6. QRS(space for saying QRS)
7. TUVW(space for saying TUV)
8. WXYZ(space for saying WXYZ)
9. Now, I know my ABC'(space for saying—Now, I know my ABC's.)

In a good program, the user will apply all three approaches (affirmations, positive statements, and instructive statements) to form a learning sequence that will impact the mind.

Chapter Fourteen

Last Step—Changing Who You Are

*If you don't like something change it;
if you can't change it, change the way you think about it.*
Mary Engelbreit

We have learned to be who we are. So, if we are not happy with who we are, we can change ourselves—word by word, thought by thought, and act by act—through the use of positive, affirming *programs*. Note, I stress the word *program* to imply a series of affirmations, positive statements, and instructive statements, built around a central theme.

People do not realize the impact on our mind, body, and emotions by just one simple thought. Even though positive affirming statements are simple in nature, they profoundly influence our systems and the energy that flows within our bodies. Positive thoughts of joy, happiness, fulfillment, achievement, and worthiness create positive results. A book by John-Roger and Peter McWilliams entitled <u>You Can't Afford the Luxury of a Negative Thought</u> explains:

Negative thoughts bring negative results—dislike, indifference and withholding; disease, poverty and misery; fear, lack and alienation.
and
You may have a habit of negative thinking, built up over years of repeating negative thoughts. This repetition has made the habit strong.

The authors explain that thoughts create physical reality—not instantly but eventually. The same is true of my programs which create subtle changes that occur over time. Suddenly, you wake up one morning and realize that you are different—that you have changed. The approach follows an effective formula:

- Positive words create positive thoughts,
- Positive thoughts create positive feelings,
- Positive feelings create positive emotions, and
- Positive emotions create mental and physical well being.

In the beginning, focusing on the positive may be difficult; it may, in fact, seem almost impossible. The way to change thought patterns, however, is through practice. Unlike physical exercise, if you practice too much, you seldom wake up sore the next morning. To determine if positive statements modify your emotions, try an easy three-minute exercise. Find a comfortable position, close your eyes, and slowly repeat the following statement over and over:

"I am totally at peace with myself."

You will relax and change your emotional intensity, thereby calming your mind and body. In effect, you control the climate in your mind through a positive thought process. With my approach you are going to employ approximately seventy-five positive thoughts to propel you forward.

Unsolicited Influence

The fact that your thoughts shape your emotions is a critical consideration. Sometimes, we do not realize when we are being influenced. During my years in education, I worked for a person who had an unusual quirk. When he was trying to make a point, he would snap his thumb and little finger together. The following year, I was working on my doctoral degree and while standing with a group of colleagues, I found myself in a position of elaborating on an idea. During the process, I snapped my thumb and little finger. When I realized what I was doing, I stopped and blurted out, "Oh, no!" They asked what was wrong. I apologized and continued explaining in my normal fashion. Later, with time to reflect, I knew that I had internalized what I considered a bad habit. Throughout our lives, we are constantly being programmed by information and events we may not wish to internalize.

Children are easily influenced by negative programming. Obviously, parents and family have the strongest impact, but our schools have the potential to shape the emotional health of young people, as well. Being a former educator, I am quite aware of the possibility. If a school has a negative environment, the possibility exists for children to develop feelings of inadequacy and inferiority. In education, we are concerned about the gap between what a child knows and what he should know. The tactics which teachers use to close the gap shape children, and the students may view the learning moments as either positive or negative. Unpleasant experiences may cause unsolicited but powerful internalization of the recollections. Pressures to excel, over-crowded classrooms, difficult assignments, coercion from peers, expectations from society, the need to achieve, and other stresses are compelling influences on our youth. Obviously, we need positive reinforcement programs that start in the home and continue in school. It is the *obligation* of parents and educators to insure that children are exposed to a nurturing environment.

Chapter Fifteen

When You Should Use the Program

> When we are no longer able to change a situation,
> we are challenged to change ourselves.
> **Victor Frankl**

To Begin the Day

Let's assume you have developed or purchased a program and you are ready to begin. You are probably asking yourself when is the best time of the day to use the program. Of course, your particular work, school, or family schedule will dictate time to some degree. Many people wake up "blue" in the morning and have trouble "kick starting" themselves to get underway. Using the programs early in the morning is one option. As I have stated, "positive words create positive feelings," so ask yourself how you wish to wake up every morning. You can start your day by saying either, "Good morning, Lord! What a beautiful day!" or "Good Lord, it's morning and another blooming day." It is your choice.

When I was in the Marines, serving as a chauffeur for various officers, I was told by my commanding officer that it was critical every morning for me to greet the individual I was picking up in a positive, happy and enthusiastic manner. I was reminded that, more than likely, I was the first person the officer would meet and my attitude would set the tone for the rest of the day. As a result of past habits, today, I often set my tape/CD program to use as the alarm. When the alarm goes off, I wake up to a positive, assuring program. I get up talking to myself as I shave, shower, and make the bed. By then, the program has finished, and I am off to a wonderful, positive and constructive day. Beginning your day in such a manner will pay big dividends.

While Driving

Later, sometime during the day, usually while driving in the car, I like to play the same tape/CD in the background. I am not necessarily listening to the tape/CD but I know my subconscious mind is taking note. Some would call this use of the program a subliminal approach to listening. I have had a few laughs with this approach because several years ago, cell phones were not popular. Several users were self conscious about driving down the road talking to themselves. I can remember pulling up to a stoplight. The person in the car next to me looked over and smiled as I continued talking to myself. If you think you will be self conscious, I suggest holding a cell phone so that you give the appearance of conversation. Another opportunity may be to play the same tape and quietly listen to what is being said. I like the idea of playing the program just before going to sleep. My machine shuts off automatically, and I get additional, positive influence at the end of my day.

You should be creative and try whatever fits your schedule or location. Remember the twenty-one day principle—if you miss a day, add two additional days to your schedule to insure the reinforcement of necessary programming.

With Exercise Programs

Another good time to use the program is while you are exercising—running, jogging, walking, and the rest. If you have used it earlier in the day, just listening to the recording will help reinforce what you have already programmed.

If you are incorporating the recordings into a school activity, such as baseball, football, cross-country, track, or golf, use the program just before you begin your exercise or training. I recall reading about one the world's greatest athletes, Jim Thorpe. The Olympic team was headed overseas aboard ship—they did not travel by airplanes during his day—so during the sunlight hours, everyone would work out and actually practice various events. Thorpe, on the other hand, would sit and contemplate. His thought processes were similar to the tape programs because he would think positively and visualize what he planned to accomplish. After a period of time, he would begin to practice. More than most, Thorpe understood the importance of mental preparation and was often criticized for his reflections. Today, Bobby Knight, a successful basketball coach, has commented that in sports, the mental factor is four to one over physical skills.

For Subliminal Reinforcement

Most of the time, people respond to my question "what does subliminal mean to you," with comments such as "it is something subversive." Subliminal messages need not be subversive; they may in fact be positive. No matter, in our everyday lives we receive subliminal messages almost every minute, unaware of how much they affect our subconscious mind. Subliminal is defined as *below the threshold of our consciousness*. The messages we receive bypass the conscious levels of our mind and shape the subconscious.

Subliminal messages are too faint or too fleeting to be noticed by the conscious mind but evoke a response in the subconscious mind. I incorporated a subliminal message in my recording series in the following manner:

- The positive statement was repeated in the pause between messages when you verbalize the statement.
- Later, the volume of the message in the pause was reduced so that you would not hear the statement, making it subliminal or below the hearing threshold.

Subliminal messages occur in your environment below normal sounds, yet are picked up by your subconscious mind. For instance, you may react to your name or other information about you if someone is talking in an adjacent room. Your subconscious will alert you to the incident. Often, people go into the adjoining room to see what is being said. After regular use of a recording, you can simply play the same program, not worrying about whether you are hearing it, letting it program you subliminally. You can turn on the recorder and lower the sound so that it will not interfere with what you are doing. When using my programs, your subconscious mind hears the subliminal message, as well as the intended message, thus providing further reinforcement to your long-term memory.

When the Subconscious Mind Never Sleeps

Our conscious thoughts and activities shut down and do not operate when we are asleep. The subconscious mind, on the other hand, never sleeps. Years ago, I tried to program my mind with messages at night when I was sleeping—something I would not recommend. I could never fall into a deep sleep because my subconscious mind was always listening to the recorded programs. I experimented with subliminal programming during the daylight hours and found that I experienced little peace. My head was always hot and my brain activity was always on high alert.

Consequently, I recommend that you actively use one fifteen-minute program per day and use the recording as a subliminal device sometime later in the day. Your subliminal use should be limited to fifteen minutes so it will not disturb concentration and peace of mind. If you wait for four hours between programming, you can use the tape as a learning tool, listening to the program and doing mind talk. Mind talk, as mentioned earlier, entails your saying the words and phrases in your mind without repeating them out loud. If you become distracted during the program, do not worry, just keep the tape running, remembering that your subconscious will continue learning.

Using Multiple Repetition

The reason I have included subliminal messages on the recordings is simple. Approximately, 75 to 80 messages exist on a program. If 75 is multiplied by 21 (the number of days that the program should be used), you will hear the messages a total of 1575 times. Because you are saying the messages 75 times and hearing one subliminal message for each statement, the total becomes 225 messages per day (75 + 75 + 75 = 225). In a twenty-one day period, you have bombarded your subconscious with 4725 messages. You will have achieved one necessary ingredient to change thoughts—repetition. Although not essential, passively listening to the program one more time each day provides additional subconscious indoctrination. You compound the reinforcement to approximately 9450 times.

Simple repetition becomes redundant and most of us do not like to continue with a project for long if it is constant repetition. Our minds will kick into resistance very quickly if the right design, content, and proper attention span are not built into the program.

During Meditation

The programs lend themselves very nicely for use as a meditation tool. The way to use the approach is without voice (mind talk). We do this all the time but in this instance, the situation is controlled. After soothing your mind for meditation, turn on the tape, and quietly listen to the program. If you do not want to do the exercise with mind talk, simply relax, concentrating on the quiet, mellow experience that will unfold. At the end of the recording, you will have completed fifteen minutes of meditation. If you so desire, shut the tape off and transcend into a deeper reflection.

As you can see, the recordings allow for flexible use. A statement made by one participant named Jeff explains:

You don't realize what you've got until it's gone. I missed a day of listening to the Enriching Relationship tape and the following day when I started again, it was just like a wave of calm passed through me, relaxing me, making me feel very comfortable. Now, I know how much the tape was doing for me in ways that I didn't even consider.

Be creative and try the approaches, adjusting them to fit your particular schedule.

Chapter Sixteen

Conclusion

There is a certain relief in change, even though it be from bad to worse! As I have often found in travelling in a stagecoach, that it is often a comfort to shift one's position, and be bruised in a new place.
Washington Irving

Final Suggestions

When I first discovered the method in 1993, I was its biggest skeptic. My questions concerned the short length of the program and the simplicity. On the other hand, because of the way I developed the concept, I knew that it was much more than what appeared on the surface. Later, when I completed the first stage of research with friends and clients, I begin to understand that this was not an ordinary concept. The approach was indeed special. It offered a positive way to change lives. Most of all, I recognized that the fifteen-minute tape or CD was a pleasant, relatively easy, and positive experience, something I wished for everyone. After years of use by numerous participants, I am convinced that this subtle, long-term, positive approach will change the user.

In 1993, I needed to change my personal life in regard to relationships, finances, health, and most of all, peace and tranquility. If I were to describe the program's power, I would say it altered the inner me more than I could ever imagine. Changing the outer shell is easy. We can loose weight, color our hair, wear different clothes, use makeup, have a face lift, or work on any part of our physical appearance, but in the end, we have not really changed who we are inside.

My approach will alter your belief systems, help you mirror to the world a more charismatic self, "jump start" your day, create *triggering devices* that cause you to think in a more positive manner, change the chemistry of your body, help you develop healthier habits, and create subtle, long-lasting internal growth. You will find that your emotions and feelings become more wholesome. You will begin to manifest what you want in life.

The programs are simple to design and develop.

One key ingredient is needed, to believe that it will work. Do not bother to be the skeptic that I was—don't reinvent the wheel. Experience the positive programming and you will wake up months later to find that your life has changed. In fact, you will be in awe of the changes.

Decide what you want—select a program or design a program—watch the "world of your mind" grow and change.

It is my hope that you spend time reading and re-reading the book. The research studies revealed many key issues that will help you change. Make sure you know and understand the "mind resistance" concept. Ask yourself some of the following questions:

- How am I "mirroring" myself to others?
- Am I paying attention to my "mind talk" and "mind chatter?"
- Do I understand my "sponsoring thoughts?"
- What "triggering devices" do I want to possess?
- What program will "jump start" my day?
- How will I use my programs to the maximum benefit?
- How am I being programmed by incidental "subliminal" programming at work, play, or in my family environment?
- What "voice commands" do I want to give myself each day?
- Do I have internal dialogue that is negative and needs changing?
- Are painful thoughts of the past haunting me?
- Do I have forgiveness issues?

- Am I manifesting into my life those negative programs? (Programs you really do not want but are destroying the real you.)
- Are my feelings and emotions negative?

This portion of the book was written after the disastrous terrorist attacks of September 11, 2001. The event only highlights the need for a more charitable world. Recently, conversations between neighbors, among family members, and in the media tend to concentrate on global problems. We find it hard to believe that civilized people hold such anger, animosity, and hatred toward each other. I can think of no better way for all of us to help create a more positive world than to be positive ourselves. To provide an inspirational influence, we should spread more happiness, love, caring, joy, and peace. My recommendation is to assist a church or charity with worthwhile endeavors. Join a civic group, such as the Lions Club whose motto is WE SERVE. Start making an impact on the world. You will promote an end to the negativity that exists in society by simply mirroring to the world happy, positive thoughts toward yourself and mankind. Helping others is a wonderful way to end absorption with your own concerns and to realize the blessings that you have in life.

Concerns

There are four basic concerns to consider before and during the use of the programs. The first concern results because the programs put you in a positive, peaceful state of mind. Once you feel good about yourself, you are tempted to stop using the programs. (Remember surprise benefit number one—early on, almost everyone felt peace, tranquility, and a sense of wellness.) Since the program is so powerful, you should be encouraged to continue, not cease. It is not hard—only fifteen minutes a day.

The choice is yours but always remember your long-range goal—to engrain the new positive statements into your subconscious mind. Reprogramming or altering your subconscious belief system takes time, so be aware that you may become complacent. Make using your programs part of your routine and remember the benefits you are receiving.

A **second major concern** relates to the mind resistance problem. Many people do not pay attention to this detail and fight using the programs from the very start. Learning about mind resistance was a major find in my studies and should help you understand what you need to do to change yourself. Fight the urge to stop—keep going! I promise that the benefits will be enormous.

A **third concern**—write down in detail the condition of your life before you begin the recordings. Since the programming is so subtle, you may fail to recognize the benefits because you are changing engrained subconscious thoughts that are not easily detected. If you continue use, eventually you will notice that your life has changed. These subtle changes creep up on you without your awareness. Because your belief systems have been altered, the positive changes will continue.

Fourth and lastly, negative changes may seem to occur. For instance, you may desire prosperity, so to advance your situation; you must change your current employment, venturing into something totally different and new. Embarking into unknown territory may appear to be negative but in reality, it is a positive step, necessary to achieve more financial prosperity. Even though it may be fun and exciting, starting a new enterprise is stressful. A new learning curve begins, causing you to go through added stress to achieve your goals. Something that seems negative, at first, eventually becomes positive.

If a person is in a negative relationship and improves her self-esteem, she will want to make some positive changes. She realizes that she needs to get out of the relationship, knowing it is not healthy for her She makes the decision, only to find that she misses the person—something entirely normal because she has disturbed her comfort zone. She may even feel lonely and frightened. The break up may appear negative, at first, but is necessary for her to have an opportunity to grow as a person and discover a rewarding relationship. Six months later, she will begin to see it as a positive benefit. When you change your belief systems, expect other changes to occur in your life—changes that result as a byproduct of your new beliefs. The choices you make will be for the better. You must take charge of your life to manifest your dreams and change the "world of your mind"—one positive word at a time.

Your mind is like fertile soil, whatever seed you plant, will grow.

P.S. The Last Surprise!

As I wrote the final chapter, I still needed a title for the book. For a starting point, I checked with several of the book companies on the web and typed in the word *miracle*. I had tentatively decided on the title, <u>The Fifteen-Minute-a-Day Miracle</u>. I was searching to learn if anyone else had a similar name, so I was looking for books with the word miracle in the title. During the search, I bought two books, <u>The Greatest Miracle in the World</u> by Og Mandino and <u>A Course in Miracles</u>, distributed by the Miracle Distribution Center.

Surprisingly, the *Voice* offered me the answer. I found that there are similarities between <u>The Greatest Miracle in the World</u> and my ideas. The book implies that if you read a twenty-minute memorandum every night for 100 days, you will change your life for the better. Sound familiar—change your life in twenty-minutes a day vs. fifteen-minutes a day. In the introduction to the <u>Course in Miracles</u>, Helen Schueman and Bill Thetford explain their discovery. Helen told Bill that she felt she was about to do something very unusual, yet neither one had any notion what that was to be. On a night in October, it happened. She telephoned Bill in a panic and related how her **"inner voice"** would not leave her alone. She followed the **"inner voice"** and the <u>Course in Miracles</u> evolved. In the Introduction of this book, I describe my experience with an "inner voice" and my development of the first program on relationships. The discovery in the <u>Course in Miracle</u> follows a similar pattern. The incident definitely caught my attention, compelling me to focus intently on the task at hand. Ultimately, I followed the "inner voice" that guided me to the completion of my first recorded program.

Now, as the old saying goes, "the ball is in your court." It is your turn to use and share the fifteen-minute miracle. In view of the fact that the most important factor in your life is YOU, it is time to take responsibility. In his didactic poem "Invictus," William Ernest Henley wisely concludes:

I am the master of my fate;
I am the captain of my soul.

Appendix A

Programs in a Series

The mind is dynamic and capable of multi-tasked activities. Information is received, stored and used every millisecond of the waking day at a conscious level. The subconscious mind does not sleep and even during slumber is using mind information to produce such things as dream thought.

Consequently, it usually takes more than just one tape/CD program to create major, permanent change. The various series listed below offer twenty-one days of programs with five in a group or 105 days of continuous programming around a central theme.

Listening to the introduction/instruction tape or reading the book is a must before starting any program.

The Power Pack Series:

The following are the fifteen series and the purpose behind each concept:

Personal Growth Series

1. Power Pack Series One—A Fundamental Necessity. Addresses the fundamental areas of need for most individuals.
2. Power Pack Series Two—Wellness for Life. Helps users concentrate on improved, overall health.
3. Power Pack Series Three—Enriching Relationships. Helps you build stronger, richer and deeper relationships.

Addiction Series

4. Power Pack Series Four—An Independent, Self-Determined Life. Designed for those struggling with codependent patterns.
5. Power Pack Series Five—Tobacco Free for Life. Designed to touch on all areas that will contribute to kicking a tobacco addiction (great supplement for any type of stop tobacco habit program).
6. Power Pack Series Six—Weight Management for Life. Designed to help you develop a more positive "mind set" around the subject of weight loss (good to use if you are on any of the multiple diets on the market today).
7. Power Pack Series Seven—Ending Chemical Dependency. Addresses and supports the "one-day at a time concept" advocated by AA to end chemical dependency.

Sport Series

8. Power Pack Series Eight—Basketball—Hoop it Up. Contains the sport series for basketball to improve the mental approach to the game.

9. Power Pack Series Nine—General Athletic Competence. Designed for the general sport enthusiast or beginner in any sport who wants to start strengthening the inner self in areas of confidence, self-acceptance, desire, dedication, determination and more.
10. Power Pack Series Ten—A Better Game of Golf. Addresses the mentally challenging and individual sport of golf.

Emotional/Mental Health Series

11. Power Pack Series Eleven—Stable Mental Health. Touches on improvement in a wide range of mental health issues.
12. Power Pack Series Twelve—Life after Divorce. Designed to help millions of individuals that go through divorces.

Career Improvement/Business Success Series

13. Power Pack Series Thirteen—Improving Sales Power. Helps improve selling power and the personal skills required in this highly mental endeavor.
14. Power Pack Series Fourteen—Business Success. Promotes a variety of skills necessary to be a successful, happy, and responsible manager or worker

Children's Series

15. Power Pack Series Fifteen—A Great Beginning. For children ages 4-12.

Note: Power Pack Series may repeat a program. For example—Self-Acceptance is a program appropriate to many of the Power Pack Series. We present detailed information the first time a program is described. Later references do not repeat the specifics.

Dr. Harlan Fisher

Personal Growth Series

Power Pack Series One

A Flourishing Life

"A simple, clear and practical guide to positive change for everyone."

The Power Pack Series One programs were chosen because they focus on those areas in which most people want help and/or get stuck and need help. They are core areas of life: self-acceptance, health, prosperity, relationships, and forgiveness, and contain a cross section of important concepts, such as energy, confidence, integrity, strength, sex, organization and more. The specific programming will give an individual over 105 days of continued learning.

Program Descriptions:

A HEALTHY ME. When you've got your health, you've got everything! Through the positive affirming statements in the tape, watch how a positive attitude toward your health and body will increase your energy level, minimize illness, and maintain a healthy vitality. *"I have a lot of energy;" "I create my own future;" "I deal honestly with my sexuality;" "I eat good nutritional food;" "I am a wonderful miracle and creation."*

ENHANCING PROSPERITY. All action begins with a thought. Reprogram your self-limiting thoughts and open doors to prosperity and riches. Learn to see yourself as a prosperous person, and you will begin to take the actions necessary to make the thought a reality. *"I claim my prosperity;" "I am receiving prosperity daily;" "I am a child of fortune;" "I have emotional prosperity;" "Money is attracted to me;" "Prosperity means health, peace, joy and love."*

RELEASE AND LET GO—FORGIVENESS. We cannot achieve total peace of mind and joy if we cannot release a grudge or anger toward those who have wronged us. In order to achieve complete joy and satisfaction in our own lives, we must learn to let go and forgive. *"I learn from forgiving others;" "When I forgive I feel healthier inside;" "There is no limit to my forgiveness;" "I forgive all who have ever harmed me;" "Peace on earth begins with me I forgive;"*

IT'S OK TO BE ME—SELF-ACCEPTANCE. When you accept yourself as a positive, powerful being, you have taken the first giant step toward a rewarding and fulfilling life. Reprogram your subconscious mind to get rid of the negative programming that is holding you back. This tape will empower you with feelings of self worth and point you in a direction to achieve all of which you are capable. *"I am me;" "I am a very special person;" "I am the only me that will ever be;" "I am a confident and incredible person;" "I am exciting and special;" "I am a healthy vivacious* person."

ENRICHING RELATIONS. Stop hurting those closest to you. Use this tape to start building long lasting relationships with everyone you encounter. Start living a happy, more fulfilled life, centered on the ones you love the most. *"I radiate love and understanding;" "I am a positive caring person;" "I am loving and affectionate;" "I commit easily to my relationships;" "I create fulfilling relationships."*

Power Pack Series Two

Wellness for Life

Power Pack Series Two concentrates on the areas of a concern for most people—better overall health and the core topics of energy, ideal weight, sex, growing younger, and illness-free bodies. Positive thoughts and feeling have a direct correlation to the overall wellness and health of your body, so it is a must program for someone who desires balance, harmony, and physical and mental health.

Program Descriptions:

A HEALTHY ME. When you've got your health, you've got everything!

FOUNTAIN OF YOUTH—GROWING YOUNGER. Aging is something you learned to do. Start undoing all the fallacies associated with aging and start growing younger in your mind. Extend your health and youthfulness beyond what is normally considered possible. Learn seven important lifestyle habits that will improve your longevity. Begin to bring laughter, youthful thinking and high productivity back into your life. *"I am as young as I think I am;" "I learn to grow younger;" "I will never retire—I love work and life;" "I am a timeless person;' "I feel young and enthusiastic."*

LIGHTEN UP—WEIGHT LOSS. Eliminate those self-defeating eating habits and replace them with healthy, positive thoughts. This program is a must for anyone trying to lose or maintain weight. Start developing healthy self esteem messages, making it possible to lose weight easily and naturally—and keep it off! Great for use in conjunction with any weight loss program when your ultimate aim is to program your mind to keep the weight off permanently. *"When I eat I conquer my past;" "Healthy food makes me beautiful;" "I eat in a relaxed manner;" "I deserve to be trim and healthy;" "I eat nothing but low-fat, nutritional foods."*

GET INTO THE FLOW OF LIFE-ENERGY. Think with more energy! Learn to recharge yourself naturally and have energy. Feel your spirit lift as you face each day with a renewed zest for life. Feel energy surging through your body as you accomplish more each day with extra joy and vigor. *"I have an exciting highly energized, happy life;" "I have high emotional feeling about life;" "My strength and endurance is awesome;" "I have built up a strong energy reserve;" "I am calm, cool, collected, wide awake and full of energy."*

ENHANCING MY SEX LIFE. Sex is a natural, normal part of your daily life. This tape will help you overcome many of your sexual limitations and give you supporting, affirming information about how you can achieve a more natural and positive view on sex. Feel at ease with the opposite sex and put an end to self-sabotaging behaviors, which cause loneliness. *"Sex is a beneficial part of my life;" "I deal honestly with my sexuality;" "I give myself permission to have appropriate, safe sex;" "I like to feel pleasure and sexual energy in my body;" "I am a highly sensuous, sexual person."*

Power Pack Series Three

Enriching Relationships

Power Pack Series Three will help you build stronger, richer and deeper relationships with those you care about. Develop harmony and satisfaction and start living a happy more fulfilled life, centered on the ones you love the most. The core concepts introduced center around your self-acceptance, developing relationships, interpersonal skills, a healthy sexual attitude, setting boundaries and limits, and if you are single and dating. Supporting, affirming statements focus on intimacy, acceptance, trust, attraction, sharing, forgiveness, serenity and much more. Develop the relationship you have always dreamed of—and start right now. Stop hurting those closest to you.

Program Descriptions:

ENRICHING RELATIONS. Stop hurting those closest to you.

IT'S OK TO BE ME—SELF-ACCEPTANCE. When you accept yourself as a positive, powerful being, you have taken the first giant step toward a rewarding and fulfilling life.

SETTING BOUNDARIES. Take over your life and begin anew. Start by setting boundaries, which are healthy and appropriate for you. Learn to set limits on what you will do for others and will allow others to do to and for you. Let others know and respect the boundaries you set for yourself. *"I accept responsibility for who I am right no;" "I take care of myself one day at a time;" "I allow people to operate within the limits I set;" "I have perfect harmony and balance in my life;" "I am an incredible, healthy, dynamic and loving person."*

DEVELOPING INTERPERSONAL SKILLS. Have a dynamic relationship with everyone you choose. Learn to communicate at a deeper emotional level that will ultimately foster open communication with others. Become a receptive listener and unleash incredible feelings of self-confidence necessary to foster the kind of close relationships you so desire. Gain a deeper understanding of others with skills to achieve mutual understanding at a higher level than ever before. *"I am a positive person and good listener;" "I speak with authority;" "I am self assured;" "I watch and read the listener's body language;" "The tone of my voice reflects what I feel."*

ENHANCING MY SEX LIFE. Sex is a natural, normal part of your daily life.

Dr. Harlan Fisher

Power Pack Series Four

An Independent, Self-Determined Life

This series is designed for those struggling with codependent patterns, but is also for individuals who occasionally find their boundaries crossed, have trouble releasing the past, or find themselves giving up their personal power and becoming a "rug" (letting people walk all over you). Stop being a victim and begin to create healthy relationships. The programs selected for Power Pack Series Four all center around the conceptual framework of boundaries, letting go, living our lives, recovering from addictions and self-acceptance. Learn that you cannot control others, only yourself. Concentrate your energies on your own responsibilities and choices in life. Learn to set limits and develop personal boundaries to be more positive and effective in your own daily life. Start taking care of yourself in the truest sense and bring happiness back into your life.

Program Descriptions:

IT'S OK TO BE ME—SELF-ACCEPTANCE. When you accept yourself as a positive, powerful being, you have taken the first giant step toward a rewarding and fulfilling life.

LET GO OF THE PAST—START LIVING MY DREAMS. Learn to let go of the past and the future and live your life in the here and now. Move forward toward greater peace and serenity. Concentrate your energies on that which you have the power and responsibility to control. Start taking care of yourself in the truest sense of the word. *"I am independent and take care of myself daily;" "I focus on the present moment;" "I am happy and think and act in ways that enhance my life;" "My happiness and well-being comes from within me;" "I accept life's difficulties with serenity;" "I let others deal with their own lessons in life;" "Each day I move closer to greater peace and harmony."*

CHOICES—I CHOOSE MY DESTINY. No one can make your choices for you. Your choices are yours and yours alone. Learn to make important choices, which ultimately change your life. The ability to make choices is one of your greatest personal powers. Take that power and direct your life. *"I choose today an make my own future;" "My choices are mine and mine alone;" "I make my own decisions in life;" "I choose to have a healthy attitude about life;" "I am a by-product of my choices;" "I choose to live in the present moment."*

SETTING BOUNDARIES. Take over your life and begin anew. Start by setting boundaries, which are healthy and appropriate for you.

LIVING MY LIFE. Learn that you cannot control the lives of others and begin to concentrate on your own responsibilities and choices in life. Taking care of yourself physically, mentally, emotionally and spiritually is extremely important. Start learning today to live your own dreams and begin to shape your own life. *"I am growing in serenity and self love daily;" "I am in control of my own life;" "I no longer feel lost and alone;" "I enjoy my time alone;" "I have miracles in my life;" "I am peaceful, warm and loving;" "I love who I am and enjoy myself."*

Power Pack Series Five

Tobacco Free for Life

Have all your attempts at breaking the tobacco habit failed? Learn to control the urges associated with using tobacco. Start manifesting those healthy attributes you so desire. Powerful affirming statements about energy, health, vitality, strength, skin tone, breathing, control and overall feelings of well-being are presented, starting you on the way to reprogramming those negative damaging habits. Enjoy freedom from your addiction and feel more alive with more energy than ever before. Start kicking the habit today with this powerful series.

Program Descriptions:

KICK THE TOBACCO HABIT—TOBACCO FREE. This program contains all the elements necessary to program your mind to think healthy. Experience the feelings of pleasure and satisfaction that come when you develop the freedom of a healthier life style. Powerful affirming statements start to reprogram those negative, destructive thoughts that keep you from being the person you always knew you could be. *"I now have a new exciting life;" "I am determined to be free;" "I do not dwell on my urges;" "I protect* and respect my body;" "I am strong and enjoy my new exciting life;" "I reward myself in other healthier ways now."

IT'S OK TO BE ME—SELF-ACCEPTANCE. When you accept yourself as a positive, powerful being, you have taken the first giant step towards a rewarding and fulfilling life.

GET INTO THE FLOW OF LIFE—ENERGY. Depression, stress, improper eating habits, anxiety, a lack of joy in your life, all contribute to a low energy flow within your body.

A HEALTHY ME. When you've got your health, you've got everything!

RECOVERING FROM ADDICTIONS. Stop being a victim and begin to create healthy, positive habits, which are personally fulfilling. Learn to be the one who controls your life and makes it the dream life you always wanted. Free yourself from the past and the future and start living in the moment. *"I am alive, wide awake and free to have a good life;" "Today I open myself to new belief;" "Today is a day of healing for me;" "I feel joy and peace in the present moment;" "I make my dreams and wishes come true;" "I choose the direction I want my life to go."*

Power Pack Series Six

Weight Management for Life

Most weight loss programs fail! They fail because the mind has not developed a permanent "mind set" around the concept of controlling your weight. Manage your addiction to eating with this program, affirm your mind, and attain your ideal weight. You need an overall healthy, balanced program around the concepts of weight loss, self-acceptance, energy, and recovering from addiction. If you are tired of failure alter your mind with successful thoughts that will assure success in your weight loss program. One simple program will not work; you need to bombard yourself in all these areas—get your mind to believe it, so you will succeed.

Program Descriptions:

LIGHTEN UP—WEIGHT LOSS. Loosing weight is difficult but if you are on any kind off weight loss/weight watch program, affirming the mind is critical to your success. This program is a must for anyone trying to lose and maintain his or her weight. Self-fulfilling concepts help you overcome the addiction to eating and will start you on the way to a life-long slim/trim program. Your health is critical to your happiness, relationships, success and overall abundance in life. Take advantage and start developing healthy self-esteem messages, making it possible and easy to lose weight easily and naturally—and keep it off! *"I eat low fat nutritional foods." "I am trim and healthy;" "When I eat properly I conquer my past;" "Healthy food makes me beautiful;" "I deserve to be trim and healthy;" "I am a trim, slim, healthy and dynamic person."*

IT'S OK TO BE ME—SELF-ACCEPTANCE. When you accept yourself as a positive, powerful being, you have taken the first giant step toward a rewarding and fulfilling life.

GET INTO THE FLOW OF LIFE-ENERGY. Think with more energy! Learn to recharge yourself naturally and have an abundance of energy.

A HEALTHY ME. When you've got your health, you've got everything! *creation."*

FOUNTAIN OF YOUTH—GROWING YOUNGER. Aging is something you learned to do. Start undoing all the fallacies associated with aging and start growing younger in your mind.

Power Pack Series Seven

A Life without Chemical Dependency

Millions of Americans suffer from some kind of chemical dependency, either alcohol or drugs. Age is no predictor and dependency starts as early as elementary school. Start saying NO to DRUGS.

Program Description:

RECOVERING FROM ADDICTIONS. Stop being a victim and begin to create healthy, positive habits, which are personally fulfilling. Learn to be the one who controls your life and makes it the dream life you always wanted.

IT'S OK TO BE ME—SELF-ACCEPTANCE. When you accept yourself as a positive, powerful being, you have taken the first giant step toward a rewarding and fulfilling life.

LET GO OF THE PAST—START LIVING MY DREAMS. Learn to let go of the past and the future and live your life in the here and now. Move forward toward greater peace and serenity.

SETTING BOUNDARIES. Take over your life and begin anew. Start by setting boundaries, which are healthy and appropriate for you.

LIVING MY LIFE. Learn that you cannot control the lives of others and begin to concentrate on your own responsibilities and choices in life.

Sport Series

Power Pack Series Eight

Basketball—Hoop it Up!

Power Pack Series Eight is all about basketball. This series contains one tape/CD over basketball and four supporting programs over energy, confidence, self-acceptance, and being a super learner. The theory behind this series is that the technical elements of any sport can be taught to almost anyone with athletic ability. All great athletes have one thing in common—strong mental ability. Having mentally engrained confidence into your mind will assure you of a higher level of playing ability that will complement your natural abilities. The series is ideal for elementary, high school or college athletes.

Program Descriptions:

BASKETBALL—HOOP IT UP. What does it take to be calm, cool, collected and have the ability to follow through when the pressure is the greatest? This program contains self-acceptance, confidence, energy, strength, team building and technical information helpful to athletes competing in basketball. *"The basketball and I are one;" "I shoot the ball in a deliberate fluid motion;" "I am peaceful and calm on the basketball court;" "I hit all of my shots;" "My persistence and determination work miracles for me."*

CONFIDENCE—THE WINNING EDGE. Hal Bock from the Associated Press wrote about a conversation he had with Pat Williams, senior Vice President of the Orlando Magic. Williams related comments from B.J. Armstrong who had played with Michael Jordon during his career with the Chicago Bulls. B.J. said that Williams had forgotten the most important thing about Michael Jordon. Jordon had the ability to focus, block out all distractions, and concentrate his abilities. He was always in the moment. He could seal off the past and not worry about the future. Michael's self-confidence showed in his enthusiasm and excitement for the game. He had an internal passion that exuded confidence. This program is all about the necessary qualities for establishing an internal trust to build self-assurance, persistence, focus, determination, and intensity. *"I am intense, focused and confident of my abilities;" "I am focused and trust my instincts;" "I inspire others with my confidence;" "I am a decisive confident person;" "I play exceptionally well under pressure."*

IT'S OK TO BE ME—SELF-ACCEPTANCE. When you accept yourself as a positive, powerful being, you have taken the first giant step toward a rewarding and fulfilling life.

GET INTO THE FLOW OF LIFE-ENERGY. Think with more energy! Learn to recharge yourself naturally and have all the energy you need.

SUPER LEARNER—IMPROVED LEARNING. Originally this tape was designed to help my daughter Katie and insure that she would have healthy thoughts about school and learning. Anyone who has trouble with any part of learning or the school environment can profit from this tape. We all have negative thoughts about learning that create anxiety, frustration and anger. Start propelling yourself into a new dimension and overcome learning resistance. *"Nothing is too hard for me to learn;" "I have good healthy study habits;" "I am an intelligent wise person;" "Learning comes easily and naturally for me;" "The more I read the quicker I learn;" "I enjoy school and learning."*

Power Pack Series Nine

General Athletic Competence

Power Pack Series Nine is designed to help players involved in athletic programs of any kind. It contains supporting tapes about general athletic programs, energy, confidence, self-acceptance, and being a super learner. Athletes who are involved in any type of sport, who like sports or who are preparing to play a sport in school will profit from this series.

Program Description:

A BETTER ATHLETE. Developing desire, dedication and determination is not easy and deserves your attention. This program concentrates on general attributes that will help enhance athletic performance and help maintain focus and motivation in any sport undertaken. *"I choose to be a great athletic;" "I have intense concentration;" "I stay focused and play with intensity;" "I am a smart, and alert team player;" "I have strengths and talents that are unique."*

CONFIDENCE—THE WINNING EDGE. This program is all about the qualities that one needs to establish the internal trust to build self-assurance, persistence, focus, determination, intensity and self-confidence.

IT'S OK TO BE ME—SELF-ACCEPTANCE. When you accept yourself as a positive, powerful being, you have taken the first giant step toward a rewarding and fulfilling life.

GET INTO THE FLOW OF LIFE—ENERGY Think with more energy! Learn to recharge yourself naturally and have all the energy you need.

SUPER LEARNER—IMPROVED LEARNING. Originally this tape was designed to help my daughter Katie. This was to assure that she would have healthy thoughts about school and learning. Anyone who has trouble with any part of learning or the school environment can profit from this tape.

Power Pack Series Ten

A Better Game of Golf

Power Pack Series Ten is all about golf. Golf is a challenging and individual sport that requires a lot of mental activity. Because golf is a thinking sport more than a power sport like boxing—golf rewards patient players. All great athletes have one thing in common, strong mental ability. Having this engrained into your subconscious will assure you of a higher level of playing. This series has a program on golf plus supporting tapes over energy, confidence, self-acceptance, and super learner. Being a super learner is included because athletes spend a lot of time working out, often need help on the academic portion of their studies, and must constantly learn how to improve their game. This series is ideal for elementary, high school, college athletics and the general public.

Program Description:

IMPROVING MY GOLF GAME. Golf is like life there is always more to learn. One of the great things about life and golf is that they are always challenging. Golf requires a great deal of mental ability and is considered one of the thinking sports. In every step of the game, patience, perseverance, preparation, and strategy are required. Because golf is a mental game, players must develop a positive attitude toward the game. This program is all about mental attitude and basic skills necessary to be successful. *"I love the game of golf;" "I have a curse strategy and control my mind;" "My golf swing is a thing of beauty;" "I always play the high percentage shot;" "I control my emotions on each shot;" "I am consistent and pay attention to little details;" "I am positive and have a great mental attitude."*

CONFIDENCE—THE WINNING EDGE. This program is all about the qualities that one needs to establish the internal trust necessary to build self assurance, persistence, focus, determination, intensity and self-confidence

IT'S OK TO BE ME—SELF-ACCEPTANCE. When you accept yourself as a positive, powerful being, you have taken the first giant step towards a rewarding and fulfilling life.

GET INTO THE FLOW OF LIFE-ENERGY. Think with more energy! Learn to recharge yourself naturally and have all the energy you need.

SUPER LEARNER—IMPROVED LEARNING. Anyone who has trouble with any part of learning or the school environment can profit from this tape. We all have negative thoughts about learning that create anxiety, frustration and anger.

Emotional/Mental Health Series

Power Pack Series Eleven

Mental Health for Life

Everyone usually experiences some kind of mental health issues. We all have days when life seems overwhelming. Sometimes this overwhelmed feeling is related to stress, low self-acceptance, anxiety, depression or mind/body healing problems. These can be situational in nature where once the cause is removed we come back into internal balance. This tape is designed to offer a wide range of mental health issues that can help as supplemental support during these situational distressing times. The programs of about stress, self-acceptance, healing, anxiety, and depression, all offer support around these issues.

Program Description:

IT'S OK TO BE ME—SELF-ACCEPTANCE. When you accept yourself as a positive, powerful being, you have taken the first giant step towards a rewarding and fulfilling life.

HEALING—MIND AND BODY. Feeling good mentally and physically is a blessing, and as the old saying goes "when you have your health you have everything." The body and all its cells are powerful natural healing mechanisms that are activated as we think and speak. This program will help your mind and body by developing positive thoughts around good mental and physical health. *"I release the healing power of my body;" "I give attention to healthy loving ways;" "Happy thoughts create a happy body;" "My body is healing itself constantly;" My body is a beautifully designed healing force."*

LET IT ALL HANG OUT—ELIMINATE STRESS. Most stress is caused by lifestyle problems, such as diet, exercise, smoking, job-related issues, family situations and life in general. Stress is the overall response of the body to any strong demand made upon it, emotionally or physically. This program was designed to give you positive statements that will address most of the major areas that cause stress in your life. *"I am in control of my life;" "I enjoy my relationships with my family and friends;" "I discuss family problems calmly and peacefully;" "I lead a healthy and productive life;" "I take time every hour to relax and breath deeply;" "I set and maintain priorities."*

ANXIETY—NO FEAR OR WORRY. Fear and worry create anxiety. We become so overwhelmed with life that our coping skills are not strong enough to help us with the unease. When we are in a state of anxiety, we need help dealing with these fears and worries. This tape was designed to give you positive affirming statements that will create calm feelings to reduce your sense of anxiety. *"I have a wonderful life;" "I love to work and be around people;" "I see the good in everything and everyone;" "I am totally in control of my life;" "Living life is a beautiful experience;" "I choose to live a fully, happy and productive life."*

DEPRESSION—COME BACK TO LIFE. Depression can be situational in nature or a serious mental disorder. An estimated 10-14 million people in the United States suffer from some level of depression. This program is designed for the individual experiencing situational depression or who is on some kind of medication, either doctor-prescribed or over-the-counter. It will act as a good supplementary program to go along with whatever activity or treatment you are undertaking. *"Life is exciting and wonderful;" "I am a kind and forgiving person;" "I am happy and loving all the time;" "I* have wonderful feelings about life;" "My spirits are always high;" "I am the most positive person I know;" "I am always looking for something new."

Power Pack Series Twelve

Life after Divorce

Power Pack Series Seven was designed to help the millions of individuals that go through divorce each year. Going through a divorce is probably one of the more difficult times in life. Much support is needed in the areas of forgiveness, self-esteem, relationships, health, and dating. Each tape also contains sections of other concepts about interpersonal relationship skills, confidence, strength and integrity. It is a must tape for anyone going through a divorce or who has just gone through a divorce.

Program Description:

RELEASE AND LET GO—FORGIVENESS. We cannot achieve total peace of mind and joy if we cannot release a grudge or anger toward those who have wronged us *on*

IT'S OK TO BE ME—SELF-ACCEPTANCE. When you accept yourself as a positive, powerful being, you have taken the first giant step toward a rewarding and fulfilling life.

ENRICHING RELATIONS. Stop hurting those closest to you. Use this tape to start building long-lasting relationships with everyone you encounter.

A HEALTHY ME. When you've got your health, you've got everything!

PREPARING FOR A DATE. Eventually, dating begins again after a divorce and can produce high anxiety and dread. All kinds of negative feelings usually surround dating. Therefore, many individuals need positive affirming statements to help them begin a new transition and to overcome many of the self defeating feelings of poor self worth that may occur in the wake of a divorce. *"I am liked, lovable and loving;" "I am adorable and charitable;" "The opposite sex like who I am;" "I treat the opposite with* respect;" "I am always relaxed around my date;" "My date always finds me attractive."

Career Improvement/Business Success Series

Power Pack Series Thirteen

The Winning Edge in Sales

Selling any product requires strong self-esteem and mental toughness. The series concentrates on sales power but is appropriate for anyone whose work involves contact with the public.

Program Description:

Selling—Sales Power. This is definitely a twenty-one day program. All the positive statements contained in this program are necessary and important to have engrained into your mind. The program contains important statements about prospecting, making a presentation, overcoming objections, enthusiasm, and other sales-related topics. *"I am always prepared to meet the public;" "I love meeting and selling people;" "I present good ideas and suggestions;" "I make good sales presentations;" "I believe in my products and services;" "I am always positive and upbeat."*

IMPROVING ORGANIZATIONAL SKILLS. This program is for anyone who wants to have a sense of being in control through organizational management. Studies have shown that successful people pay close attention to all details in the organizational process The statements collected are appropriate for any endeavor in your life, whether it be school, business, family, athletics, church or the multitude of activities in which you might be involved. *"I am organized and pay attention to details;" "I plan my day and work my plan;" "I have improved and plan my day accordingly;" "I plan my day around my priorities;" "My life is calm, peaceful and simple;" "I develop a to-do list of activities;" "I have a lot of self-discipline."*

CAREER—HAPPINESS AT WORK. It seems that almost everyone complains about his/her job or career! The people who are happy and love their jobs tend to be the people who become more successful. This program is designed to help you reach better job satisfaction and hopefully a more satisfying career. *"I am happy in my work;" "I am stimulated at work;" "I look forward to going to work;" "I am energized at work;" "I always finish my work on time;" "I admire the people I work with;" "I care about those in the work place."*

CONFIDENCE—THE WINNING EDGE. This program is all about the qualities that one needs to develop the internal trust necessary to build self assurance, persistence, focus, determination, intensity and trust in your self-confidence.

IT'S OK TO BE ME—SELF-ACCEPTANCE. When you accept yourself as a positive, powerful being, you have taken the first giant step toward a rewarding and fulfilling life.

Power Pack Series Fourteen

Lifelong Success in Business

Managing or working in any business environment requires many different skills. This program is built around the areas of happiness at work, interpersonal skills, organizational abilities, confidence, and stress eliminators. Any worker can profit from the program, whether in management or hourly-employed. It will help to propel you to a higher level of thinking about your role in the work environment.

Program Description:

CAREER—HAPPINESS AT WORK. It seems that almost everyone complains about his/her job or career. Why is there such unhappiness in the work place? Most of our lives are spent earning money to get what we want out of life. The people who are happy and love their jobs tend to be the people who become more successful.

DEVELOPING INTERPERSONAL SKILLS. You can have a dynamic relationship with everyone you choose. Learn to communicate at a deeper emotional level that will ultimately foster open communication from others. Become a receptive listener and unleash incredible feelings of self-confidence necessary to foster the kind of close relationships you so desire. This program will help you gain a deeper understanding of others. *"I am a positive person and good listener;" "I speak with authority;" "I am self assured;" "I watch and read the listeners body language;" "The tone of my voice reflects what I feel."*

IMPROVING ORGANIZATIONAL SKILLS. This program is for anyone who wants to have a sense of being in control through organizational management. Studies have shown that successful people pay close attention to all details in the organizational process. The statements presented are appropriate for any endeavor in your life whether school, business, family, athletics, church or the multitude of activities in which you might be involved. *"I am organized and pay attention to details;" "I plan my day and work my plan;" "I have improved and plan my day accordingly;" "I plan my day around my priorities;" "My life is calm, peaceful and simple;" "I develop a to-do list of activities;" "I have a lot of self-discipline."*

CONFIDENCE—THE WINNING EDGE. This program is all about the qualities that one needs to develop the internal trust necessary to build self assurance, persistence, focus, determination, intensity and self-confidence.

LET IT ALL HANG OUT—ELIMINATE STRESS. Most stress is caused by lifestyle problems, such as diet, exercise, smoking, job-related issues, family situations and life in general. Stress is the overall response of the body to any strong demand made upon it, emotionally or physically.

Power Pack Series Fifteen

Children's Edition

A Great Beginning

The power pack series for children are similar to the adult series but are shorter in time, only 8 minutes, and the statements are simple and concise. The programs will help your child develop a healthy, positive attitude about the subjects presented.

Program Descriptions: The programs should be explained to your child before beginning.

SELF-ACCEPTANCE—I AM ME. This program will empower your child with feelings of self worth and point him/her in a direction to achieve his/her potential. It should fit into almost any program series you are trying to develop for your child. *"I am a very special person;" "I feel sure of myself;" "I approve of who I am;" "I am a nice person;" "I feel good about myself."*

I HAVE GOOD FRIENDS. This program is good for helping children work on building relationships, whether with parents, other children, siblings, teachers, or others important to the child. Help the child learn not to hurt his/her loved ones. Help your child start building long-lasting relationships and friendships. *"I am a caring child;" "I am a joy to be around;" "I am a very happy person;" "I am a caring child;" "People like who I am;" "I am open and receive love easily."*

I HAVE CONFIDENCE. This tape is all about the qualities that a child needs to build self-assurance, persistence, focus, determination, intensity and self-reliance. *"I am a confident student;" "I believe in myself;" "I am determined;" "I like who I am;" "I trust in myself;" "Others can rely on me;" "I am beautiful and valuable."*

I AM A SUPER LEARNER. Start propelling your child into a higher dimension of learning and help him/her overcome learning resistance. *"I feel happy and believe in myself;" "I like learning new things;" "I am a good student and I write well;" "I read and study well;" "I am a quick learner;" "Studying is fun to me."*

HAVE A GREAT DAY. When your child cannot muster positive feelings due to difficult circumstances, he/she needs a "jump start." As your child starts using the program, after about four or five minutes a change occurs, and the child attitude begins to transform from negative to positive. *"Life is exciting;" "I am having a great day;" "I smile and laugh a lot;" "Loving myself is good;" "I am kind and loving;" "I love who I am;" "I am a warm and special person;" "I have power over what I think."*

Any of the above programs can be purchased by contacting Dr. Fisher at mediapmf@gmail.com.

Appendix B

Individual Programs For Your Consideration

By now, you possess all the information you need to design your own personal programs. However, remember Surprise Benefit Seven and what it states. When using the twenty-one day plan, participants found that they were able to expound on the statements, individualizing them. You, too, can use the programs in the same manner. Simply pick out the ones which fit your desires or needs and use the programs, knowing that you will personalize them and toward the end, they will be yours.

The topics that follow include all those listed in the preceding chapters and more. Pick what you like and design your own program or contact Dr. Fisher at—mediapmf@gmail.com.—for information on how you can purchase what you desire. The programs are listed under the same themes as the Power Pack Series. Additionally, other single topics are located in the back of this chapter.

Personal Growth Programs
Jump Start your Day
Self Acceptance
Relationships
Energy
Forgiveness
Prosperity
Health

Addiction Programs
Addictions
Boundaries
Choices
Let go of the Past
Tobacco Free
Weight Loss
Sports Programs
General Athletic Program
Basketball
Confidence
Golf
Emotional/Mental Health Programs
Improving Sensuality
Preparing For A Date
Self Relaxation
Anxiety Free
Coping with Death and Dying
Eliminating Stress
Healing The Mind And Body
Depression Free
Coping With Grief
Career Improvement/Business Success
Happiness At Work
Improving Interpersonal Skills
Becoming A Super Learner
Sales Power
Getting Organized
Children's Programs For Adults
Disciplining My Child
Children's Programs—ages 4-12
Golf
Super Learner
Enriching Relationships
Confidence
Self Acceptance

Personal Growth Programs:

JUMP START MY DAY

When we think a positive thought, a different chemistry takes place in our bodies. To begin days with positive chemistry, we can try a "kick start" program. Many times negative information coming from our jobs, family, children, or finances create the need for some positive feelings. When we cannot muster positive feelings due to these circumstances, we need a "jump start". Use this program in the morning before starting your day or any time life seems out of control or depressing. I found that as you start using the program when depressed, it is hard to feel optimistic, but four or five minutes into the program, a change occurs from negative to positive. There can be no cause without an effect. A positive thought must create a more positive reality.

I have taken four positive statements from twenty different programs so that all areas of your life should be covered.

I radiate love and understanding; I am a positive caring person; I am a very happy person; My life is very harmonious; Life is exciting and energizing; I relax and am very calm; I give and accept love easily; I like being an active person; I am at peace with myself; All is well, all is love; Love is the best gift I can give; I live today with joy and love; I am a positive person; I create my own future; I am energized and love my work; I radiate good health and vitality; I appreciate my uniqueness; I know sex is natural for me; I like to touch and be touched; I have a healthy sexual desires; I trust myself; I am a powerful person; I choose my words wisely; I am an attentive and focused listener; I am confident when I speak; I release and accept help into my life; I have power over my thoughts; All changes I make are for the better; I have a healthier, happier way of life; I am as young as I think I am; I live a joyful, fun life; I have a zest for life; I feel young and exciting; My life is carefree and simple; I care about myself; I am calm, peaceful and serene; Exercise is fun and enjoyable; What a lovely world I live in; My feelings are changed for the better; I am a warm, special and unique person; I am a lot of fun to be with; I am a very special person; I like life; Everywhere I go I go with love; I am a prosperous person; I am rich, well and happy; My potential to achieve is unlimited; I have a peaceful harmonious life; I am successful in everything I undertake; I welcome this new day; I have strong internal powers; I claim and affirm my own goodness; My mind and body are calm and peaceful; I laugh and smile easily; I celebrate myself today; I am in control of my life; I love who I am and enjoy myself; I have miracles in my life; I am peaceful, warm and loving; I accept my own personal growth; I deserve to be happy and I am; I love and care for myself; Loving myself is very healing; I am kind and loving; I am a perfect, whole, and complete person; I am strong emotionally; I find the source of my well being within myself; I enjoy experiencing life; I accept all good things into my life; I see all the beauty around and within me; I love and feel good about myself; Each day is a new blessing in my life; I am responsible for my own life; I control my own destiny; Life is exciting and fun; I trust, honor and respect myself; I am whole, perfect and complete in every way; I have true self-love; I control my own feelings and reactions; I choose how I feel; I appreciate my abilities; I am an unlimited person; I am thankful for my good mind; I am liked, lovable and loving; Life is fantastic.

SELF ACCEPTANCE—I AM ME

When you accept yourself as a positive, powerful being, you have taken the first giant step toward a rewarding and fulfilling life. Love yourself and begin to act from the "mind power" of free choice. Reprogram your subconscious mind to reject the negative programming that is holding you back. This tape will empower you with feelings of self worth and point you in a direction to achieve all of which you are capable. This is a tape that should fit into almost any program series you are trying to develop.

I am a very special person; I live in the present moment; I am a warm. special and unique person; I like life; I smile a lot; I am exciting and special; I am somebody important; I am a positive person; I love myself; I like who I am; I approve of who I am; I am a confident incredible person; I am a lot of fun to be with; I am enthusiastic and full of energy; I am a very intelligent person; I like other people; Other people like me; I am always full of life; I like how I feel and think; I am very special and believe in myself; Who I am makes a difference; I have unlimited potential; I am a warm and sincere person; I am a clever person; I am strong and secure; I think good thoughts; I am proud to be me; I have a can do feeling; I feel sure of myself; I like who I am right now; I like how I do things for myself; I approve of who I am; I have talents and skills; There is a glow around me; I am so glad to be alive; Good things radiate from me; I am a very special person; My mind is quick and alert; I make things work for me; Others find me attractive; I am warm, sincere, honest and genuine; I recognize and appreciate my strengths; I am lovable worthwhile and capable; I like who I am and I am glad to be me; I am more acceptant of myself and others; I am more and more in charge of my life; I am constantly changing for the better; I have a sense of purpose in my life; I have a sense of excitement in my life; People like to hear what I have to say; There is no one else like me in this world; I discover new talents about myself daily; My self confidence and self esteem are awesome; I have a sense of purpose and excitement in my life; I have a lot of personal power and self confidence; I feel good about myself; I love and appreciate myself; I draw to myself caring friends; I have beautiful personal qualities; I have skills and talents that are unique; I am an incredible confident person; I have a lot of energy and a can do attitude; Who I am makes a difference; I am the only me that will ever be; I am a healthy vivacious person; I appreciate all that I learn; I appreciate all my blessings in life; I deserve everything I create; I have powerful inner strengths; I am an exciting person to know; People like to know what I think; Others find me easy to be with; Every day is a new exciting beginning; I allow others to get to know me; I am filled with positive self confidence; I deserve everything good in life; I am a sensuous passionate person; I have a lot of energy and vitality; I am an intimate, passionate loving person; I would rather be me than anyone else; Everywhere I go, I go with love.

ENRICHING RELATIONSHIPS

This program is good for working on any kind of relationship. Stop hurting those closest to you. Reprogram your mind with positive thoughts about personal relationship values. Start building long lasting relationships with everyone you encounter. Begin living a happy, more fulfilled life centered on the ones you love the most.

I am a caring person; I radiate love and understanding; I accept others for who they are; Others accept who I am; I am a forgiving person; I have been forgiven by everyone; I am a gentle loving person; I accept love easily; I draw loving people to me; I radiate the feelings of love; I laugh easily; I like to smile and laugh; I am a joyful person to be around; I am a very trustworthy person; Others like me because I am affectionate; I am a positive caring person; I am fun to be around; I am patient and kind; I am easily satisfied; I am a very happy person; I accept my partner; I trust my partner; I am honest with my partner; I am a good listener; I love my relationships; Others care about me; My life is very harmonious; I am a very happy person; I am happy about my life right now; I love life to the fullest; I naturally like others; I am accepting of others; I am a love magnet; I am a fun person to know; Life is always good to me; I am open to receive love; I give love unconditionally; Others love and trust me; I attract people to me; I am an interested listener; I am an open and honest person; I like to communicate well; I am a kind and gentle person; I am an easily satisfied and happy person; Others like me because I radiate love; I am an easily satisfied and happy person; I enjoy fulfilling relationships; I have a joyful fulfilling relationship; I am trustworthy and a positive person; I accept and forgive others; I can be loved by others; I am loving and affectionate; I give love and kindness to others; I respond to my partners needs; I deserve satisfying relationships; I have a committed relationship; I commit easily to my relationships; I am able to have rich relationships; I am a kind, strong and loving person; I listen well when others speak; I understand others needs; I am open to receiving love by everyone; I love to touch and be touched; I enjoy hugging others; I am loving and attract people to me; I receive much affection and love; I am a wonderful and kind person; My life is happy and full of joy; I am content with myself and others; Each day life gets better and better; I create fulfilling relationships; I am open and receive love easily; I am an understanding and kind person; Others naturally like to be with me; I am a person who attracts love and harmony; I am absolutely a loving person; I am a naturally loving and beautiful person; I generate much love and caring form everyone; Others are kind and good to me; I appreciate all my relationships; I am committed to all my relationships; I freely give my love unconditionally; I am a good listener and communicator; My relationships become more rich every day; I see myself enjoying my relationships; I have the power to have dynamic relationships; I am known for my caring and kindness; I love the highest and best in all people; I now draw the highest and best people to me.

GET INTO THE FLOW OF LIFE—ENERGY

Depression, stress, improper exercise, poor eating habits, anxiety, and a lack of joy in your life contribute toward a low energy flow within your body. Think more energy! Learn to recharge yourself naturally and have all the energy you need. Feel energy surging throughout your body as you accomplish more each day with more joy and vigor than ever before. Develop the zest for working, playing, loving, and living by increasing the flow of vital energy within your body.

I have all the energy my mind and body needs; Today more than ever I can feel energy flowing in my body; I feel a rush of energy throughout my body;

Life is exciting and energizing; I have drive and desire and am fully energized;

I am a highly energetic person; I always have a maximum energy flow; I am fit, eat well and enjoy life daily; I have a strong sense of control and direction in my life; I live totally and completely in the present moment; I trust my own ability to live a rich and happy life; I form new and exciting relationships daily; I have high emotional, energizing feelings about life; I am fully aware and live life to the fullest; I improve my energy flow daily I am honest with myself and follow my feelings; I transcend myself and allow new experiences to enter my life; I always utilize my maximum amount of energy; I have vigor, drive and a love for living; I am sure of myself and enjoy the changes life offers; I take time to enjoy life—I am at peace; I have a peaceful, pleasurable stress free life; I have good relationships and a stress free happy life; I am physically, emotionally and mentally energized; I relax and am very calm in all situations; I have a very relaxed, peaceful approach to life; I am a happy, outgoing, productive, and fun loving person; I am happy with life and enjoy change; I live peacefully and quietly enjoying the present moment; I have more than enough energy to achieve my goals; I am highly energized and live life with a lot of zip; I feel peaceful after a full hard day at work; I relax after a physically active event; I am physically fit and enjoy good nutritional eating habits; I am whole, perfect and complete in every way; I always stay rested, sleep deeply and remain physically fit; I never allow anything to disturb my serenity in life; My total body works in harmony with itself; My strength and endurance is awesome; Exercise is an important part of my daily life;. I have an enormous amount of physical, mental and emotional energy; I live a balanced social, physical, political and domestic life; I have built up a large strong energy reserve; I exercise aerobically every other day for twenty minutes; I like eating slowly a good balance nutritional meal; I have fresh vegetables and fruit in my diet daily; I count my sugar and fat intake all the time; I am calm, cool, collected, wide awake and full of energy; When I am excited my energy flows and I become renewed; A balanced meal assures me of more energy; All my body's organs work in perfect harmony with each other; I am growing younger and younger each day; I am always alert, vital and energized; Life is so exciting; I have a positive attitude about life and follow a good eating plan; I can feel all my cells vibrating in unison with energy; I take the proper vitamins and minerals; I drink fresh, pure, highly energizing water; I am responsible for my own behavior, feelings, actions and attitudes; I meditate and work on maintaining a calm me;

I have reduced my salt and sugar intake; I eat very little saturated fat and red meat; I take care of myself by enjoying life, exercising and eating well; I find time to be quiet and relax; I express myself in music, art, dance, sports and hobbies; I am happy and find it easy to laugh; I enjoy walking, riding my bike, running or swimming; I eat a balanced diet and enjoy a variety of fresh natural foods; I eat three well balanced meals daily; I eat foods high in nutrients and low in calories; I enjoy my relationships with all living beings; I like talking about how I feel and think; I find all people interesting and enjoyable; I give and receive love easily; I always do what I need to do now in the present moment; I plan my day around work, sleep, relaxation and family; I am always highly energized and enjoy life to the fullest; I often close my eyes and scan my body for physical or mental signals; Any form of recreation increases my energy supply; I enjoy and have my own total fitness program; I have a lot of physical, mental and emotional energy; Meditation helps me release tension in my mind and body; Stretching exercises are good tension reducers; I stay away from junk food knowing it robs me of energy; I relax and take time to think, play and laugh; My days are full and exciting and full of energy; I have a lot to look forward to every day; I like being an active person; I love my adventurous, highly energized life.

RELEASE AND LET GO—FORGIVENESS

We cannot achieve total peace of mind and joy if we cannot release a grudge or anger toward those who have wronged us. Let go of thoughts and feelings around anger, blame, mistakes, hurts. Use your own "mind power" to release. Begin expressing love and forgiveness for yourself and others. In order to achieve complete joy and satisfaction in your own life, learn to let go and forgive.

I am at peace with myself; I forgive my mother and father; I am a peacemaker; I count my blessings; As I love, I am loved; As I forgive, I am forgiven; I am a very forgiving person; I send love to everyone; I am flexible, I forgive; I learn about life when I forgive; When I forgive, I am giving of myself; All is well, all is love; I forgive anyone and anything in my past; I am the master of forgiveness; The divine in me forgives myself; The divine in me forgives others; I release all blame toward others; Others like me because I am forgiving; I am a totally forgiving person; I learn from forgiving others; I forgive myself and enjoy peace within; I do not judge myself or others; I forgive those who were thoughtless; When I forgive I feel healthier inside; I release resentment toward others; I release all animosity toward others; Love is a great healer so I forgive; There is no limit to my forgiveness; Love is the answer to my every need; Love is letting go of fear I forgive; I look for the good I forgive others; I am at peace because I forgive others; I am a good communicator and listener I forgive; I treat everyone with love and respect; I have personal integrity I forgive; When I forgive I am giving and receiving; Peace on earth begins with me I forgive; I forgive and live in the present moment; The moment is what counts I forgive; I have no resentment or blame for anyone; I am ready for the greater good in my life; I forgive those who hurt me in any way; Forgiveness helps build my self esteem; I thank everyone for my experiences in life; I am in harmony with life because I forgive; I am receiving all the forgiveness I deserve; I share my happiness with others; Love is the best gift I can give; I am renewed and transformed; I forgive myself and live in harmony; I expect miracles daily I forgive; I forgive all I have resented in the past; I love everyone who ever disappointed me; I release all blame and resentment; My life is better than it has ever been; All the wonders I seek are within me; I change the impossible to the possible; My environment is a mirror of my attitudes; I enjoy life to the fullest I am forgiving; I am better every day because I am a forgiver; I love everyone including myself; I live today with joy and love; I am in charge of my life so I choose to forgive; I forgive myself for everything I said or did that I regret; I always expect the best for me; I release beliefs that keep me from being forgiving.

PROSPERITY—I CLAIM MY PROSPERITY

All actions begin with a thought. Learn to become rich within your mind. Reprogram your self-limiting thoughts to ones that will open doors to prosperity and riches. Learn consciousness of prosperity and become a person who thinks smarter, works less and achieves more prosperity in every avenue of life. You will begin to take the actions necessary to make that thought a reality. Prosperity is one of the areas in which I have found more mind resistance, so beware.

I am a prosperous person; I think and live prosperity; I love being prosperous; I love money; Money is good; I use money wisely; I am receiving prosperity daily; I am receiving riches; I am a child of fortune; I deserve prosperity; I claim my prosperity; I desire and I receive all kinds of prosperity ; I daily grow prosperous; Money is attracted to me; Riches flow into my life; I have health prosperity;

I am blessed with riches; I attract what I desire; I know that I am wealthy; I am rich, well and happy; My thoughts are on having plenty; I give to others; I have emotional prosperity; I have financial prosperity; Whatever I ask for I receive; Money is flowing into my life daily; I easily create lots of money; I am a powerful money magnet; I am thankful for my success; Wealth is created in my mind; I handle large sums of money; My mind dwells on prosperity; I am not limited by anything; I am willing to have what I want; I am a magnet that attracts good things; My love is a prospering truth; I wish prosperity for everyone; I love money and money loves me; I grow more and more prosperous; I live in an abundant universe; Lots of money flows into my life; I am full of successful thoughts; I think healthy, radiant thoughts; Being prosperous is my birthright; Peace of mind is prosperity for me; All things I need are provided for me; Everyone loves my financial success; Everyone is supportive of my talents; My potential to achieve is unlimited; I deserve total abundance in all things; I am the most prosperous person I know; I draw to me prosperity and abundance; I am getting richer and richer every day; I am a shining example of total prosperity; I grow more and more prosperous each day; I am successful in everything I undertake; I cultivate thoughts of prosperity; I mentally accept my highest good right now; I am creating positive changes in my life; I claim my greatness in all things; Prosperity means health, peace, joy and love; I have a peaceful, harmonious life; I have a large dependable permanent income; All my financial obligations are being met; I handle all situations with self-confidence; I am in the flow of inexhaustible substance; Creating money is a fun loving venture for me; My supply unfolds at the same rate as my needs; All riches are flowing speedily into my world; I give consistently and I receive consistently.

HEALTHY ME

When you've got your health, you've got everything! The statements will affirm a positive attitude about your health and will increase your energy level, minimize illness, and maintain a healthy vitality.

I have a lot of energy; I am a positive person; I honor and care for myself; I meet my own needs daily; I am the master of my life; I exercise daily; I eat good, nutritional food; I create my own future; I feel good about myself; I have high personal integrity; I enhance my feeling of well being; I create comfort and a sense of well being; I am a healthy, vivacious person; Sex is a beneficial part of my life; I deal honestly with sexuality; Sex is healthy for me; I give myself permission to have sex; I have a positive attitude about my health; I think healthy thoughts; I feel stronger and stronger every day; I am growing younger daily; I am able to relax deeply; I have seven to eight hours of restful sleep nightly; I am at peace with myself; I feel fully energized every moment of my day; The present moment is my point of power; I approach life with a sense of adventure; I have strong personal power; I open to my inner power; My body works in harmony with itself; I feel alive and full of energy each morning; My sense of well being grows stronger each day; I am whole, perfect, and complete in every way; I have a sense of well being within me; I have no physical limitations; I have beautiful skin and good body tone; I eat well balanced healthy meals; I love all parts of my body; I feel peaceful and energized; I am a happy, joyful, fun loving person; I am in charge of my life; I give thanks for my health and well being; I express the child within me; I am filled with energy right now; I am a wonderful miracle and creation; I am energized and love my work; I embrace life and participate in life to the fullest; I am willing to grow and change; I listen to my body signals; I am trim and healthy; I feel and look better when I exercise; I eat health nutritional foods; Healthy, nutritional food makes me beautiful; I have a healthy life style; I eat healthy foods at work; I have created a trimmer, happier, healthier me; I lose weight easily and naturally; Controlling my weight and appetite is easy; I radiate good health and vitality; I embrace and accept my body as it is; I am the most important person in my life; I have deep emotional feelings about myself; I have unlimited potential; I am a sexual, passionate, intimate being without guilt; I am renewed and refreshed every moment of the day; I appreciate my uniqueness; I am absolutely, unequivocally unique; Life is beautiful and I cherish each and every day; I am brilliant, gorgeous, talented and fabulous; My millions of cells work in total harmony with each other; I am an incredible, healthy and secure individual; I have personal power that is manifest in all areas of my life; I am the most important person in my life; I am open and caring toward myself and others; A bright light of energy surrounds my body; I have strength, courage and personal integrity; I forgive myself now and live in love; I grow younger and younger each day.

GROWING YOUNGER

Aging is something you learned to do. Start undoing all the fallacies associated with aging and start growing younger in your mind. Extend your health and youthfulness beyond what we consider possible. Learn seven important lifestyle habits that will improve your longevity. Bring laughter, youthful thinking and high productivity back into your life.

Dr. Harlan Fisher

I am as young as I think I am; I choose to stay young; I grow younger and younger each day; I learn to grow younger; I feel young all over; I maintain my ideal body weight; I sleep seven to eight hour per night; I am extremely healthy; I live a joyful, fun life; My mind is young and so is my body; I have many interests, one of which is exercising; I eat nutritional food in moderate amounts; I have a zest for life; I am a peaceful, calm person; I intend to live to be one hundred and thirty; All my cells work in harmony with each other; I live a natural, healthy, balanced life; I have beautiful skin tone; Medically speaking I am very young; I am a healthy optimistic person; I will never retire I love work and life; I am young psychologically speaking; I am biologically a very healthy person; I feel younger and younger each and every day; I enjoy moderate everyday exercise; I enjoy drinking appropriate amounts of water daily; My body organs work in close harmony with each other; Staying young is an important mindset that I have; I know that I will always be young in mind and body; I have a strong, lean body and enjoy exercising; I am continually learning and enjoy life to its fullest; My body and mind are tingling with excitement; I have friends of all ages; I am mentally and physically a young person; I enjoy a good breakfast every day; I drink only moderately at social events; I have faith that I have the power to stay young; I live in the present moment; Time has a way of standing still for me; I have all the time in the world; I am free to change my beliefs; I have free choice to stay young; I feel better and better every day in every way; I am the hero of my own life; Love, joy and peace of mind are mine in every way; I am a timeless person; I live life at the right pace; I am unique and have special powers; I am the person I secretly knew I was; I have my attention on what is happening now; My life is all about peace, harmony, love and laughter; My life is carefree and simple; In every way I live in a timeless way; I eat naturally and comfortably and maintain my ideal weight; I have positive exciting feeling about life; I share my positive feelings with others; I feel young and enthusiastic; I am excited about being youthful; I have spontaneity and true happiness; I am always comfortable with myself; I am a focused individual who is always happy with life; I am a focused person with a lot of energy; I like the decisions I make about my life; I have youthful, exuberant feelings; I am a loving, youthful thinking person; I excel in all aspects of my life; My dress is always youthful and up to date; I lead a stress free, peaceful life; I always exercise in a casual manner; I enjoy a humorous movie or joke; I sleep seven or eight hours per day.

Addiction Programs:

RECOVERING FROM ADDICTIONS

Stop being a victim and begin to create healthy, positive habits, which are personally fulfilling. Learn to be the one who controls your life and makes it the dream life you have always wanted. Free yourself from the past and start living in the moment. This tape is one of my favorites and could be labeled advanced self-acceptance because it contains a lot of statements that build on self-acceptance/self esteem.

I welcome this new day; Today I have a fresh start; I have wonderful expectations for this day; Today is a day of healing for me; I have healthy ideas, thoughts and emotions; I have strong internal powers; I have high hopes and dreams for today; Today I open myself to new beliefs; I am gentle with myself today; I am present here and now; I am alive, wide-awake and free to have a good life; I control my own emotions; I claim and affirm my own goodness; I appreciate my own uniqueness; My mind and body are calm and peaceful; I take time and go at my own pace; I am aware of my own feelings and my self-respect; I have the power to make all my choices in life; I trust my own thoughts and emotions today; I am confident and trust my decisions; I surround myself with people who care about me; I feel joy and peace in the present moment; I enjoy new directions and challenges; I make my own happiness and enjoy life; I am enlightened, free and exhilarated; I make my dreams and wishes come true; I take full charge of my life today; Today the present is mine, and I savor it; I choose the direction I want my life to go; I feel needed, wanted and appreciated; I let serenity flow into my life daily; I live my life with pride; I trust, relax and surrender; I handle my affairs wisely and with confidence; I have a quiet place within me; Laughter is a vital part of my life; I have clarity and order in my life; I have unlimited potential and reach my dreams; I value the uniqueness in me; I am healthy in every sense of the word; I have a strong sense of self-determination; I live a healthy, productive life; I feel a boundless freedom; I have unlimited freedom; I have unlimited courage; I have inner strength and power I am at peace; I am calm and relaxed when I am alone; I am the only me there will ever be; I am perfect and the best I can be; Being healthy deserves my time, devotion and energy; I laugh and smile easily; I am a powerful person who often asks for help; I have healthy thoughts and balanced emotions; I take full responsibility for my happiness; I am a powerful, peaceful person; I have the wisdom to think before I act; I see the very best in all people; I feel powerful today; I will share my goodness today; I take time to dream and live my dreams; I can be alone without being lonely; Today I start again, fresh, renewed, with clear thoughts; I trust myself with kindness and patience; I have wonderful feelings and emotions; I am physically, emotionally and spiritually balanced; I let the inner child emerge and enjoy life; I love and give my acceptance to everyone; I am patient and draw nothing but goodness into my life; I forgive all that have ever hurt me; I deserve what life gives to me; I celebrate myself today.

SETTING BOUNDARIES

Take over your life and begin anew. Start by setting boundaries, which are healthy, prosperous and fulfilling for you. Learn to set limits on what you do for others and will allow others to do to and for you. Let others know and respect the boundaries you set for yourself.

I claim my life right now; I am responsible for my own life; I take ownership and responsibility for who I am; I pay close attention to the limits I must set; I allow people to operate within my limits; I learn about my new boundaries daily; I accept responsibility for my own beliefs, feelings and actions; I take care of myself one day at a time; I have choices in my life; I am excited about the new choices I am making; I control my own destiny; I am free and make my own decisions about life; I like the new options I have available; Life is exciting and fun; I take time to be peaceful and serene; I focus on my life but help others accordingly; My interests, personal growth and life are important; I have healthy relationships, which do not stop my growth; I focus on my own growth and well being; I honor myself and take a break when I need it; I have perfect balance and harmony in my life; I value my time alone with myself; I know how to say yes and no appropriately; I like receiving and trust my relationships; I have courage to risk making decisions; I form new relationships easily; I am totally independent person; I am fully responsible for myself; I enjoy every moment of just being me; I take responsibility for my own decisions, thoughts and actions; I concentrate on my own responsibilities first; Today I will spend time and energy on myself; I have courage to risk making decisions; I like pleasing myself and enjoying the moment; I like pleasing myself; Today I will not say yes when I want to say no; I like and accept who I am; I feel warm and secure inside and know that I am loved; I stop and think before I react to others; I have the right and responsibility to care for myself; I choose to see my highest, best self today; God created a beautiful person in me; I am a healthy, whole and beautiful person; It is my right and responsibility to care for myself; I am whole and perfect by myself; I enjoy space in my relationships; I trust, honor and respect others; Others honor, trust and respect me; I choose to see my highest, best self today; I am free to disagree and to pursue my interests; I stand up for who I am and enjoy life; I control my own thoughts and actions; I enjoy my own choices, likes, dislikes and opinions; I am unique and only need my own approval; I walk my own particular path in life; I face my own life and responsibilities fully; I have strong decision making ability; Happiness comes from taking care of myself; I am close to others without losing myself; I have the right to my own opinions and feelings; I respect others uniqueness and let them be; I care for others and let them grow on their own; I belong to me and let everyone else be who he or she is; I center my universe around my world and who I am; I have true self-love; I do not need to lead or follow in my relationships; I have loving relationships with everyone; I take the time to be self-directed; I take time to think and calmly make the right decisions; I accept my responsibilities and let go of others. I am responsible for asserting myself; I control my own feelings and actions; I am assertive and know my rights as a person; I have the right to fun and good feelings; I have the right to grow and change and say no; I choose the company I want to keep; I am a whole, perfect and complete person; My health, happiness and spirituality are my responsibility; I choose how I want to feel; I always act instead of react; My feelings come from my true inner self; I feel love, forgiveness, peace and serenity; I pay attention to my inner pain and act accordingly; I focus on my true inner self; New changes and endings improve my life; I am an incredibly, health, dynamic and loving person

CHOICES—I CHOOSE MY DESTINY

No one can make choices for you. Your choices are yours and yours alone. Learn how to make important choices, which will ultimately change your life. Be in charge of your life, remembering that each and every second of your day you can make decisions that impact your life. The ability to make our own choices is one of your greatest "personal powers." Take that power and direct your life.

I am responsible for all my own choices; I make the right choices in life; I make the right choices and move on; I make the right choices and decisions; Life is about making the right choices; I am excited about the choices I make; ; I am excited about the choices and decisions I make; I trust my decision making;

I trust that the choices I make are always right; Every second I make choices about life; I choose my life right now; I choose who I am right now; Life is fun and I make the right choices; I choose correctly all the time; I make changes when needed; My choices are mine and mine alone; Everything that happens to me is of my own choosing; The truth is that in my life I make my own decisions; I choose to live my life by my choices; Choosing is one of my greatest freedoms; I exercise my right to make my choices; I exercise my right to change; I choose today to make my own future; I have free will to choose my life's directions; I like new choices in my life; I am excited about my life choices; I choose to improve my education; I choose to have better relationships; I choose to make my family positive and happy; I choose to achieve my goals; I choose to have a strong financial future; I choose to be healthy and stay fit; I choose to exercise daily; I choose to have a rewarding career; I choose to enjoy my work every day; I choose to develop my talents and skills; I choose to have a healthy attitude; I choose to be fair in everything I do; I choose to listen to others; I choose to learn from others; I choose to know that I am important; I choose to believe that what I say and think are important; I choose to see myself as being strong and worthy; I choose to have the greatest well-being; I choose to give myself time to do the things I want to do; I choose to have a productive life; I choose to care about others; I choose to be considerate of others; I choose to be friendly, open and honest; I choose to believe in others; I choose to give to myself and others; I choose to accept openly and thankfully others help; I choose to be a good friend; I choose to be financially responsible; I choose to look good, and have a good appearance; I choose to communicate my thoughts; I choose to make my choices by design; I choose to have many alternatives in life; My life is as complete as the choices I live; All my choices count; I make thousands of choices daily; I enjoy the choices I make; I feel better about all my choices; I look at my life and see the choices I have made; I know that I am a byproduct of my choices; I accomplish in life because I make the right choices; I choose to live in the present moment; I choose to be around successful people; I improve my choices daily; I re-evaluate the choices I make in life daily; I choose solid clear goals in life; I choose to live a full, happy life; I manage my life my managing my choices; I manage my choices and manage my life; I learn what to choose and how to choose; I listen to the quietest whispers of my mind and choose wisely; My intuition helps me make the right choices; I have choices in my life; I am excited about the choices I am making; I control my own destiny; I am free and make my own decisions in life; I like the choices and options I have; I enjoy my own choices, likes, dislikes and opinions; I choose happiness; I choose to be happy and productive; I choose to eat healthy; I choose the right foods for me; I make the choice to exercise and stay healthy; I choose to stay young and vigorous. I like the new options I have made; I am moving on with life.

LET GO OF THE PAST—START LIVING YOUR DREAMS

Learn to let go of the past and move toward greater peace and serenity in your life. Concentrate your energies on that which you have the power and responsibility to control. Start taking care of yourself in the truest sense of the word.

I release and accept help into my life; I am independent and take care of myself daily; I ask for and accept the help of others; I know I need the information and experiences of others; I like laughing, playing and just being with other people; I forgive myself for my past mistakes; I remember all my moments of love, kindness and generosity; I focus on the present moment; I let go and concentrate on what I can change; I only have the time and energy to be positive; I have power over my own thoughts; I am happy and think and act in ways that enhance my life; My happiness and well being comes from within me; I forgive all my grievances against others; I let go and forgive all that have ever harmed me; By forgiving, I create a more healthy me; Forgiveness opens my mind and heart to a new future; I now have healthier, new habits to rely on; I say goodbye to the past and move on to the present; I let go and discover who I am; I let go of the past and accept the new joys awaiting me in life; I accept my goodness right now; I accept life's difficulties with serenity; I let go and accept the joyful gifts of life; When I let go, I feel more secure inside; My true security lies in accepting life as it is; I let go of all judgments and give unconditional love; I concentrate on my own life and responsibilities; I have my own lessons to learn in life and act accordingly; I let others deal with their own lessons in life; I choose happiness by acting on my behalf; I react to my own feelings, not the feelings of others; Happiness is a choice I like making; I choose to live my life and work on my own growth; I like concentrating on changing myself; I let others take care of their own responsibilities; I make my own decisions and do not interfere in others decisions; I survive very comfortably on what I have;

I learn about myself by listening to myself; I am a patient and understanding person; I am a patient, kind and considerate person; I enjoy a quiet moment for it is refreshing and calming; When I am patient I become refreshed, calm and peaceful; I accept who I am; I take responsibility for my actions; I admit my mistakes and move on; I am not perfect but working on it; I concentrate my energy on my own thoughts; I accept the things I cannot control; I unconditionally accept life and stay serene; Others are perfect within themselves and I accept them with serenity; Today this moment is the only place in time that exists; I release my past and everyone in it; The past is gone, now is what counts; I enjoy experiencing each new moment; I have enjoyed the lessons in life and moved on; Positive emotions and feelings heal my physical being; I exercise often to help release my emotions; I make my life magical, No one else does; My happiness comes from the inside and not the outside; The magic of life is within me; I am open to all the things to be enjoyed in life; I am totally satisfied with myself; I regularly take time for recreation; I use my time and energy very effectively; I just enjoy a good laugh and fun and play; I care but do not become a caretaker; I have no need to control others; No one does anything to me I am responsible for my behavior; I am calm and peaceful and nothing bothers my serenity; I work toward greater health and happiness; I have a strong self—image and know who I am; I am a whole, responsible and mature individual; All changes in my life are necessary and good for me; Life is an ever-changing event and I enjoy each challenge; Old familiar attitudes, behaviors and relationships change daily; All changes I make are for the better; I make the right decisions and change easily; Each change in my life brings me closer to being a more whole person; I am excited about the decisions I make; Each day I move closer to greater peace and harmony;

I have a new, healthier, happier way of life now; I relax and let go knowing my life is in perfect order.

TOBACCO FREE

This program contains all the elements necessary to alter your mind to think healthy thoughts. Experience the feelings of pleasure and satisfaction that come when you develop the freedom of a healthier life style. Powerful, affirming statements start to reprogram those negative destructive thoughts that keep you from being the person you know that you can be. Start kicking the habit and begin to enjoy all that life can offer. The program is a great support while you are attending or using a stop-tobacco-use or smoke-free program.

I am changing my behavior; I now lead a healthier life; I enjoy my new exciting life; Exercising is fun now; I breathe easier and feel better all over; My breath smell more refreshing; I enjoy a restful nights sleep now; I forgive myself and live in the now; Water and food tastes better than ever before; I like chewing gum; I am getting thin and trim; I like low-cal snacks; I care about myself;

I am a strong person; My clothes and hair smell better now; I can now enjoy fresh air; I smell clean and fresh; I enjoy my new habits; I manage withdrawal easily; I ask for help when I need it; I do not dwell on my urges; I no longer get colds; I feel good every day now; I am so relaxed and happy; I enjoy leading a healthier life; I am calm, peaceful and serene; I have a high-energy flow now; I enjoy a lot of new hobbies; Withdrawal is not harmful; I protect and respect my body; I like to pamper myself; My circulation is improving daily; I set my own standards; I talk to my buddy daily about my new life I see the beauty around me; I am determined to be free; I am saving a lot of money now; I am excited about life; My teeth are now clean and white; I have an ample supply of oxygen now; My circulation has improved; I handle job pressure easily now; I am peaceful, calm and relaxed; Exercise is fun and enjoyable; Water and food taste so good; I drink a lot of refreshing water; I am in charge of my attitudes; Hugging is more fun than puffing; I am more in touch with my feelings now; I postpone everything but good habits; I now have normal tasting abilities; I now have a new life, I have changed; I listen to this tape when I have an urge; I am not the least bit stressed anymore; I do not have any compulsive habits; My teeth are clean and white; Exercise is fun and easy for me now; Any discomfort I have is passing away; I am strong and enjoy my new life; Withdrawal is over very quickly now; I enjoy deep breathing exercises; I am a healthy vivacious person now; I have a buddy I can rely on; I listen to this tape when I need it; My blood pressure is back to normal; I have a larger lung capacity now; I am peaceful, calm and serene; I like to relax, meditate, and read; What a lovely world I live in; I take my time and relax often; I reward myself for my progress; My teeth are free from stains; My energy and stamina are high; My body's energy increases every day; I have a plan and I follow it daily; I have wonderful, fresh smelling breath; I do simple exercises in my spare time; Many wonderful new things are happening; I can manage withdrawal, it will go away; I am in control and changing my patterns; I am gaining my freedom from addictions; My feelings are changing for the better; I feel physically and mentally better;

Walking and other exercises are easier now; I have excellent health and extra energy; I am whole perfect and complete in every way; Being alone for a few minutes is enjoyable; My day's flow smoothly I am relaxed; I treat myself by establishing new good habits; My taste buds and sense of smell are wonderful; I am sensitive to the finer vibrations in life; People around me are enjoying a healthier environment; My mouth tongue teeth and gums are healthy; I really enjoy my new life.

LIGHTENING UP—WEIGHT LOSS

Take away those self-defeating eating habits and replace them with healthy positive thoughts. This program is a must for anyone trying to lose or maintain weight. Start developing healthy, positive self-esteem messages, making it possible to lose weight easily and naturally. Great for use in conjunction with any weight loss program when your ultimate aim is to keep the weight off permanently.

I am a healthy eater; I watch what I eat; I am strong and I am doing it; I eat healthy food; I am self confident about proper eating; I forgive the past and eat healthy; Water tastes so good; I enjoy eating smaller bites and portions; I enjoy drinking water; I eat nutritionally low fat foods; I listen to my body's signals; I am trim and healthy; I chew each bite thoroughly; I drink water before each meal; I enjoy the taste of food; I get back on track easily; I eat in a relaxed manner; I feel good about myself; I feel and look better now; I plan my holiday meals in advance; I am at peace with myself; I eat only at meal times; I like to eat healthy foods; I never need one bite more; I order less when I eat out; I say yes to success in good eating; I enjoy sitting down to eat; When I eat properly, I conquer my past; I enjoy the taste of food; Controlling my weight is easy; I eat three meals each day; I can leave food on my plate; Healthy food makes me beautiful; I deserve to be trim and healthy; I have high vigor and motivation; I like learning about food and nutrition; I have a healthy life style; I am extra careful when I eat out; I take healthy food on trips; I am in control of myself when I eat; I stop eating before I am full; I take healthy, nutritional food to work; The goals I reach are up to me; Weight loss is for myself, my life, and my future; I am strong and capable of reaching my goals; I create a trimmer, happier, healthier me; I am creating a more confident me; I feel good if I need to leave food on my plate; I feel good when I am at my right weight; I enjoy a slower, relaxing way of eating; I know the difference between body and emotional hunger; I like the texture and flavor of foods; I am slim, trim, healthy and a dynamic person; I deserve health delicious foods; I shop for healthy wholesome foods; Water tends to sharpen my taste buds; I prefer water to any other drink; I eat only enough to satisfy my hunger; I have a strong healthy, attractive body; I am in control of myself when I eat; I eat right and reach my ideal weight; I chew my food and enjoy the taste; I stay with my goal of eating properly; Less on my plate means less on my waist; Eating in or out, I enjoy eating less; I never take one bite more that I should; Weight loss goals are for personal reasons; I take full responsibility for myself; No one has to help me with my goals; Controlling my appetite is easy for me; I turn mealtime into achievement time; I am reaching my goal, I am doing it; I am not tempted to take one more bite; I feel good when I eat the right food; I stop eating four hours before bedtime; Controlling my weight and appetite is easy; I drink eight glasses of water per day; I eat only enough to satisfy my hunger; I have a strong attractive healthy body; No one else can influence my eating habits; I make a shopping list before going to the grocery store; I enjoy a cool, refreshing glass of energizing water.

Sports Programs:

GENERAL ATHLETIC PROGRAM

Developing desire, dedication and determination is not easy and deserves your attention. This program concentrates on general attributes that will help enhance athletic performance and help maintain focus and motivation in any sport undertaken.

I am a great athlete; I have a love for the sport; I enjoy working out; All workouts are easy for me; I have confidence and skills; I choose to be a great athlete; I enjoy being part of the team; I am always in control of my emotions; I stay focused and in control; I am at my best when it counts the most; I keep cool all the time; I watch my breathing; I stay calm, cool and collected; I have intense concentration; I am intense and focused; I concentrate and stay focused; I always learn from my mistakes; I love working out daily; I push myself to the limit and beyond; I take extra care of my body; I eat nutritional foods; I get the right amount of sleep every night; My body feels good to me; I am strong and healthy; I pay attention to what my body is saying; My body heals quickly and readily; I stay focused and remain calm; I breathe deeply and calmly; I am constantly improving; I have natural rhythm; Working out is fun; I enjoy playing intensely; I stay focused and play with intensity; I love who I am; I play at my highest level of ability; Playing intense and focused is enjoyable; I remain calm, relaxed and confident; I am always improving; My body works in perfect harmony; I have a lot of energy and strength; I always play at my top performance; I am the greatest; I am a team player; My team mates are important; I am always considerate of my team mates; Team sports are all about cooperation; I learn all about my team members; I focus on being a team player; I stay calm, cool and collected; I am a kind considerate team member; I help my team players in whatever way I can; I am a good team player and friend; I am a smart, alert team player; I'm awesome; I like who I am; I have strengths and talents that are unique; I practice, practice, practice; I always have a smile and a kind word for everyone; I play with high intensity; I have an enormous amount of energy; I am patient and look to make the right move; I am patient with my team mates; I am open to new ways and techniques; I have the mark of greatness; I pay attention to the tempo of the game; I have speed and agility; I am in charge of my actions; I am a strong and wise person; I am totally in charge and responsible for my actions; I am a powerful athlete; I am physically and mentally strong; My team mates believe in me; I have high tolerance and patience; I have faith in my ability; I have a great athletic future; I am in great physical health; I do what is best for the team; I am developing my skills at the right pace; The best is yet to come for me; I am confident, aggressive and skillful.

HOOP IT UP! BASKETBALL

Almost anyone with athletic ability can learn the techniques of the game. However, learning the mental aspects of the game is much more difficult. What does it take to be calm, cool, collected and have the ability to follow through when the pressure is the greatest? The confidence factor comes from deep within our subconscious mind and can be learned. All you have to do is work on the positive aspects that might support and strengthen confidence. This program contains self acceptance, confidence, energy, strength, team-building and technical information helpful to anyone in elementary, high school or college.

I love basketball; I am a confident basketball player; I handle pressure with ease; I am aggressive; I am a team player; I am poised and confident; I have confidence in my abilities; I make the right choices; I choose to be a team player; I enjoy shooting free throws; Free throws are free points; I shoot free throws calmly and deliberately; I constantly work on my free throws; I always make my free throws; I stay totally absorbed in the game; I play at 100% of my ability; My thoughts are on being calm and confident; I like the action of the game; I stay calm and read the floor activity constantly; I feel the pulse of the game; I am calm and in charge of my emotions; I think before I act; I am calm and deliberate in all my actions; I always put the ball in the hoop; I shoot the ball in a fluid deliberate motion; I am always calm when I am shooting; I pass and move with deliberation; I like who I am; I have an enormous amount of energy; I have energy whenever I need it; I have energy and strength constantly;

There is no one better than me on the floor; I am in control all the time; I have a confident smile; I am intense and deliberate; I have strong inner strength; I am totally tuned in to my team mates; My team mates and I work together; I always look out for my team mates; I project confidence to my team mates; My team mates like who I am; I am confident, confident, confident; I am calm, deliberate and aggressive; I like the feel of the basketball; The basketball and I are one; I am smooth, and deliberate in my movements; I handle the ball better than anyone; Every move I make has meaning; I make moves that are deliberate and fruitful; All my moves count; I am constantly moving and passing; Every move I make is important; I am a powerful, confident person; Shooting the ball is fun and easy; I shoot the ball with confidence; I shoot the ball with confidence and assurance; I hit everyone of my shots; Passing is quicker than dribbling; I am peaceful and calm on the basketball floor; I love and accept my skills and talents; My mind is calm and quiet; I am extremely fast and move smoothly; I stay focused and calm at all times; Playing basketball is fun; I am a very disciplined person; I believe in my dream; I have excellent momentum during a game; I am patient and persevering; My persistence and determination work miracles for me; I am living my destiny by being a great basketball player; I live my life with passion, purpose and confidence; I experience the fullness of live playing basketball; I have courage and confidence; I have joy and compassion when I play basketball. I am a confident, aggressive, talented super—star.

BASIC GOLF SKILLS

Golf is a challenging, individual sport that requires a lot of mental activity. Because golf is a thinking sport more than a power sport like boxing, golf rewards patient players. This program is about developing strong mental skills, as well as basic skills that become habits. Having the mental and basic skills will make the game easier and more enjoyable. Ideally, the twenty-one day program should be used prior to playing a round of golf to give the optimal impact.

I am a great golfer; I love the game of golf; Golf is a relaxing game for me; I concentrate on the enjoyment of the game; I take time to select the right club; I position my feet properly before swinging; I always keep my eye on the ball no matter what occurs; I visualize before I swing; I am peaceful and tranquil; I am always calm, cool and collected; I am always courteous on the course; Golf is for fun and relaxation; I constantly perfect my swing; I try different clubs on the driving range; I perfect my skills with each club; I practice putting before each game; I am relaxed and watch my breathing; I mentally relax before each swing; I spend time reading the green; I pay attention to the distance factors; I have a beautiful, smooth swing; I keep my eye on the ball and swing smoothly; I have a great follow through swing; I concentrate on hitting in the sweet spot; Golf is fun and relaxing; I am always positive and have a great mental attitude; I am consistent and pay attention to the little details; I analyze the course and make wise decisions; I pay attention to my yardage book; I can choose to go for the pin or play it safe; I watch and study all the hazards; I pay attention to the wind and my lie; I choose the proper stance for each shot; I stay relaxed and focused; I study and pick the right club; I am totally focused and concentrate on each shot; I have wisdom and courage; I am always learning to master the game; Golf is challenging and fun; I am inspired to do my best; I have many triumphs on the golf course; Golf is the greatest game invented; I find golf gratifying and tantalizing; I stay focused on one thing at a time; Each shot I make has control, balance and good timing; I have good rhythmic flow in my swing; I use the proper hand position for each shot; Each shot is short term success; I control my emotions on each shot; I always play the high percentage shot; I enjoy executing a good stroke; I work on maximizing my game; My golf swing is a thing of beauty; I have the utmost confidence in my swing; I have a sound and graceful swing; I am calm, balanced with good timing; I have a course strategy and control my mind; I am peaceful, calm and assured; I stay calm and in control; I look for the successful shot; I practice, practice, practice; The royal road to success is to practice; I use good instruction, coaching and training aids; I use patience and practice persistently; I stay disciplined and calm; I always set up and address the ball properly; I take proper preparation before each game; I have concentration, desire and a will to win; Every shot I take is perfect; I have a passion for the game; I have just the right temperament to play golf; I visualize each shot before swinging; I see, feel and trust my instincts; My putter is my ally and it is a pleasure to use; The putting stroke is short and simple; I have good rhythm when I putt; I read the greens, aim the ball and putt smoothly; I have a delicate touch when I putt; I take advantage of centrifugal force; My swing is a timed force with rhythm; I have confidence and perseverance; I have confidence and ability on each shot;

Golf is a peaceful, rewarding and honorable sport.

CONFIDENCE—THE WINNING EDGE

Develop the ability to focus, block out all distractions, and concentrate on your abilities. Stay in the moment, forgetting about the past and sealing off concerns for the future. The following program is all about the qualities that one needs to assure the internal trust to build self assurance, persistence, focus, determination, intensity and self-confidence.

I am a confident individual; I am persistent and confident; I am assertive and confident; I am aggressive and confident; I believe in myself; I choose to be confident; I have a high level of confidence; I have confidence and determination; I have excellent focus; I have focus and determination; I concentrate and am focused; I am confident and focused; I am persistent and determined; I am intense and focused; I choose to be intense and focused all the time; I trust in my abilities; I am certain and assured of my abilities; I am convinced of my confidence; I believe in myself and my abilities; I am self-confident and assured of my skills; I am bold and confident; My experience helps me to become confident; I am bold, assured and confident; I have internal security and feel confident; I am internally strong and confident; I trust in my self-confidence; I am persuasive and confident; I am excited and enthusiastic; I have a passion for the game; I am focused and trust my instinct; I like who I am; I concentrate and stay focused; I pay attention to the moment; The present moment is what counts; I am the only me that will ever be; I max out all but the present moment; I control the present moment; I stay focused and play my game; I am a mentor and instructor to my team mates; I am always in the moment and play as a team mate; I practice communicating to my team mates; I love the challenges of winning and playing my best; I play intense and aggressively all the time; I stay positive and continually improve my game; I encourage my team mates to play at their best; I trust and rely on my team mates; My team mates trust and rely on me; I have the confidence to excel with my team; Winning is easy and fun; I play exceptionally well under pressure; Playing at my best is what it is all about; I have high energy and strength; I am determined to always do my best; I stay focused, calm and collected; I pay attention to each detail moment by moment; I am always calm and focused; I stay focused and follow my plan; I have high resolve and determination at all times; I calculate and make quick decisions; I am confident I make the right decisions; I decide on the right action and take it; I am a decisive person; I always make the right decisions; I am focused and make the right decisions; I am confident I make the exact right decisions; I stay confident, focused and make the right decisions; I have an eagerness and fervor for life; I am inspiring and confident: I inspire others with my confidence; I am intense, devoted and confident of my skills; I inspire others to be confident, intense and devoted; I choose to make up my own mind; I rely on my abilities and choices; I am a winner; I am confident that I will always succeed; I am a prosperous, confident and successful person; I am confident, firm and decisive; I like who I am and the decisions I make; I am the most confident person I know. I have discovered the power and confidence within myself; I trust in my own internal confidence; All of me is beautiful and valuable; I am safe, secure and a confident person.

Emotional/Mental Health Programs:

IMPROVING MY SENSUALITY AND SEX LIFE

Sex is a natural, normal part of adult life. This tape can help you to overcome some unhealthy sexual limitations and give you positive, supportive information about how you can achieve a more natural and appropriate view on sex. Feel at ease with the opposite sex and put an end to self-sabotaging behaviors which often cause loneliness.

Sex is natural; I like sex; Sex is fun; I am interested in sex; I know sex is natural for me; Sex is natural and fun; It is OK to enjoy sex; I give my permission to have sex; Sex is pleasurable; I enjoy sex with a caring partner; Sex is a beneficial part of life; Sex has a beneficial effect on my relationship; I am honest about my sexuality; I am a sexy, sensuous person; I like to touch and be touched; I like to perform sex; Sex is best with a loving partner; I deal more honestly with my sexuality; I like gaining sexual satisfaction; I am a person who enjoys healthy sex; I enjoy satisfying my partner; The more sex I have, the better I feel; It is OK for me to have sexual pleasure; I use contraceptives appropriately; Sexual pleasure is a virtue; I give myself permission to have sex; I am fully aware of my desires; I allow myself to be filled with desire; It is OK to acknowledge my need for sex; My sexual desire is increasing; Every day my erotic appetite is increasing; I have a healthy sexual appetite; Sex is for pleasure and fun; I desire sex for the pleasure I derive from it; It is OK to fantasize during sex; I enjoy my fantasies; I feel free to explore all parts of me; I do not feel anxious about my body; I love all parts of my body; I like my genitals; I am happy with the size of my breasts or penis; I value my body's tastes and smells; The size of my breast or penis makes no difference; Intercourse is not the ultimate goal; I am a beautiful person; I concentrate on all my beauty; I take good care of my body; I feel pleasure and sexual energy in my body; I naturally feel sexual stimulation; My vagina lubricates easily; My penis becomes erect when I need it to be; I like to be aroused; I am a wonderful sexual person; I am proud of my sexual role; I have the right to initiate sex; Any sexual position is OK; I assert myself during sex; I can be dominant or submissive in sex; Sexual aggressiveness is OK; I can relax and be myself sexually; I like having an orgasm; Having an orgasm is a natural body event; It is safe to lose temporary control; I experience multiple orgasms; I like to be held; I touch every part of my lovers body; I am warm and affectionate; Sex is satisfying to me; I trust myself and my partner.

PREPARING FOR A DATE

Dating can be stressful and frightening for almost everyone. With the divorce rate about 50%, a lot of people find themselves entering the dating scene later in life. All kinds of negative feelings exist; therefore, many individuals need positive, affirming statements to help overcome their self-defeating emotions. This would be an ideal program to use when preparing for a date. Remember that positive words create positive feelings.

I am a desirable person to date; I am always kind and considerate; I am a very sexy person; I am liked, lovable and loving; I love to listen to my date talk; I am a good communicator; The opposite sex likes who I am; I like myself and laugh easily; I feel great and care about myself; Developing new friends is an important part of dating; I'm a cuddler; I am a good-looking person; I have charisma; I am adorable and charitable; Life is fantastic; I am self-assured; I have personal integrity; I trust my date; I am a trustworthy date; I am a very interesting person; I am considerate on a date; As I give, I receive; I enjoy holding hands; I am a sensuous person; I love receiving flowers; I love giving flowers; I love being considerate; My body is beautiful; I accept my body as it is; I have beautiful skin and hair; I love the way I smile; Intimacy is rewarding; As I love, I am loved; The best is yet to come; The best is yet to come because I love and am loved; I am a dynamic person; I am a kind, gentle and dynamic person; I am relaxed and feel good; It is impossible for me to fail on a date; I am a beautiful person; I am a joy to be around; I can be wild and crazy on a date; I enjoy a quiet evening; I am a most valuable person; I am a valuable person who respects his/her date; Love is a great healer; I am always in charge of my life; I think and act with confidence; I enjoy whatever we do together; I live fully for each moment; I enjoy and live in the present moment; This is my winning year; I don't prove myself with sex; I have sexual boundaries; I am a sexy person with control and boundaries; I never drink and drive; I am liked for who I am; I accept love into my life; I have a wonderful personality; I radiate warmth and friendship; I love to touch and be touched; I am a sensuous person who likes closeness; I am calm, peaceful and serene; I am the director of my destiny; Happiness multiplies as I give; I am an even-tempered person; I treat the opposite sex with respect; A handshake is OK but a hug is better; I show respect with a warm, sincere hug; Great plans with action make a good time; All the wonders I seek are within myself; I see life, as I desire it to be; I am always relaxed around my date; Conversation is easy and natural for me; My date always finds me attractive; I anticipate joyously a great date; I have great dates because I know I am accepted; I live well, laugh often and love much; My life is a wonderful adventure; Happiness multiplies as I give to another; I treat my date with love and respect; I communicate love and understanding; I don't need sex to prove I am mature; I like to get to know my date as a friend; I enjoy holding hands and looking into my dates eyes; All my dates are pleasant wonderful experiences; I am a strong powerful and secure person; Love is the best gift I can give to another; Expressing love is a good stress reducer; I never force my date against his/her wishes; I like movies, fairs, concerts and other public events; I call my date immediately if plans change.

SLEEPYTIME—SELF RELAXATION

Because the program is designed to help you fall asleep, the tape/CD should only be used during periods of relaxation and never used when operating a moving vehicle. The approach is a good example of using positive, instructive statements that guide you through a whole series of events. A good time for use is just before going to sleep at night. Often, you will not hear the ending of the tape. The program can be used either verbally or through mind talk.

I am gently closing my eyes; I feel at peace with myself; I take a long deep breath through my nose; I hold my breath and count to four; I open my mouth and exhale slowly; I take a another long deep breath through my nose; I hold my breath and count to four; I open my mouth and exhale slowly; With my eyes closed I vision a beautiful summer day; A sense of peace is coming over my body; I feel at peace and good all over; I feel happy and content; Joy, peace and harmony are mine now; I am relaxed, relaxed, relaxed all over; I vision a beautiful sky and bright sun; In the distance birds are singing; All the sounds are peaceful and happy; I am relaxed and so at peace; The warm sunlight is penetrating my body; The warm sunlight is warm and protecting; I envision the light coming into my arms; I am relaxing and so at peace; The light penetrates my skin, muscles, nerves and bones; What a glorious feeling; The warm light penetrates deeper into my body; With each breath I become more and more relaxed; I am so at peace; The light moves from my arms to my chest; The light is warm and soothing; I am relaxed and feel my energy flowing; Every cell in my body is becoming relaxed; My body is becoming heavy; I cannot move I am so relaxed and at peace; I enjoy all this good feeling; The warm light moves down to my legs; The incredible light reaches my toes; I am so at peace; My body is adjusting and responding to the light; I am drifting into a deep sleep; I am having trouble keeping awake; I have this feeling of letting go; What a wonderful peaceful feeling; I am having trouble talking now; I am at peace and going into a deeper calm; A beautiful peaceful feeling is flowing through my body; I feel warmth and a soothing feeling in my body; My emotions are all calm; I am so at peace I cannot talk only listen; I feel marvelous; The light moves from my legs into my chest and heart; I feel warmer and warmer and more at peace; The light moves gently into my head; I have a warm glow throughout my body; I am so, so relaxed; My body is in perfect harmony; My neck muscles, scalp, head and brain are relaxing; I have trouble keeping awake; My cheeks and jaws are relaxed; My body feels like a warm liquid is flowing throughout; The liquid starts flowing through my toes; The liquid is absorbing throughout my body; I am going into a deep, deep sleep; I can hear my heartbeat; All my nerves and muscles are relaxed; I am warm serene and relaxed; All negativity is being flushed from my body; Gently the liquid leaves my body through my toes; I am totally and completely relaxed and at peace; I am sinking deeper and deeper into myself; I no longer have to concentrate; I hear the beating of my heart; I am drifting off into a deep sleep; All I hear now is my heart beat; I can no longer listen, my mind is too relaxed and at peace; I am drifting off into a deep, deep sleep; I have drifted off into a calm relaxing, deep sleep; I am so peaceful; I am so calm; Life is so beautiful.

zzzzzzzzzzzzzzzzzzzzzzzzz*(just joking)*

ANXIETY—NO FEAR OR WORRY

Anxiety is a term used by psychologists and psychiatrists to explain intense fear or worry, and stress is a big contributing factor. We become so overwhelmed with life that our coping skills are no longer strong enough. Troubled, worried or uneasy feelings develop. We begin to enter a state of anxiety. This program was designed to give you positive affirming statements to ease fears and worries. Remember the research. The first "surprise benefit" found that positive thoughts create a different chemistry in the body. Positive words create positive feelings and can reduce your sense of anxiety.

This program is ideal for anyone experiencing situational anxiety. If you are using a mild doctor-prescribed medication or taking an over-the-counter relaxer, this would be a great supplemental program.

I am calm; I am peaceful; I feel good today; My mind and body are relaxed; I am calm, relaxed and in control; I am a patient person; I love my life; I am in control of my life; I like relaxing music; I have a wonderful life; I have a relaxing, peaceful life; I am calm and in control; I listen quietly to others when they talk; I get along with everyone at work; People like to be around me; I stay calm and breathe slowly; I concentrate and stay calm; I am a forgiving person; I like peaceful moments; My body stays relaxed; I am focused and calm; I like a relaxing day; I stay calm and relaxed; I evaluate every situation calmly; I am a focused individual; I love myself; I am organized; I am organized and schedule my day; I feel comfortable in a crowd; I like small talk; I never worry about tomorrow; I live in the present moment; I choose to have a happy life; I have a happy, productive life; I enjoy socializing and being around people; I exercise and eat balanced meals; I get seven to eight hours of restful sleep each night; I love to work and be around people; I always enjoy finishing my work; I am peaceful, calm and relaxed; I like closing my eyes and relaxing; I like good music and meditating; I enjoy pampering myself; I let enjoy life and just let it flow; I let others control their own lives; I stay calm, cool and collected; I see the good in everything and everyone; There is a logical reason for everything; I am totally in control of my life; I am at peace and love life; I like pleasing myself; I care about myself and share with others; I have a prosperous, successful life; I have everything I need in life; I am thankful for my life; I am thankful for all that I am and all that I am becoming; I take my time and live a slow life; I have a lot of energy; I am at peace with myself and others; I let life take care of itself; I live a happy, calm and peaceful life; I enjoy planning my day; I look forward to a peaceful evening; I am the only me that will ever be; I have a lot of friends; I enjoy entertaining my friends; I love small talk and just listening; I handle all of life's situations calmly; I am healthy and enjoy exercising; I enjoy a peaceful, calm meal; I live a calm, peaceful life; Living life is a beautiful experience; I can put off today what I can do tomorrow; Life is all about living peacefully; I always make the right decisions; I like the decisions I make; My decisions are always correct; I choose to live a fully, happy and productive life;

I like who I am right now; I smile and laugh a lot; People like me because I am calm and assuring; Life is beautiful and I love who I am.

DEATH AND DYING—THE TRANSITION EVENT

Dying is an inevitable event but since the ordeal of death is new for each of us, the experience produces some interesting concerns. I like asking the following question of individuals who have a family member who is in the final stage of life: have you ever died before? This seems to have an important impact because helping someone who is at his/her final stage of life demands reflection about the event of dying. The program is designed to take into consideration the five stages of dying—denial, anger, bargaining, depression and acceptance. Mind resistance plays a big part in its use. The resistance is compounded by the first step of denial, so beware.

A part of me never dies; The eternal part of me is forever; I have enjoyed a full and happy life; I look forward to my new experience that awaits me; I am well prepared for my next new experience; It is OK to look forward to a new existence; I am ready for my transition; I have a sense of relief; I look forward to a peaceful transition; I am at peace with everyone; I have forgiven everyone who ever hurt me; To forgive is to be forgiven; I share my feelings with my loved ones; I look forward to a peaceful final life; I wish goodwill toward everyone; I am at peace with myself; I love all that I have become; I am thankful for who I am; I have been blessed in life; I share my feelings with all those I need to; All is good and all is well; I have had a good life; I am happy for the life I have lived; I look forward to peace and tranquility; I have come to terms with my reality; I am at peace with myself; I allow others to go on without me; Others have their lives to live; I take all my thoughts and memories with me; I choose to handle how I am leaving my loved ones; My spirit, mind and body are working in harmony with each other; Others understand that it is time for me to leave them; I look forward to a peaceful transition; My spirit and God are connected; The eternal me is ready to meet God; I am happy and at peace with myself; I accept where I am in life; I have great memories of my life; I appreciate who I am; I look forward to my new existence with God; Heaven is a wonderful place to be; I let go and let God; I am a loving person to the end; I am emotionally ready to let go; I am physically ready to let go; I let go and let life happen; My spirit is ready to meet God; My life has been a miracle; I have had a perfect life; I like who I have been; I have peace and tranquility;

I have God's peace that flows within me; I have been forgiven by God; God and I are becoming one; I look forward to being with my father God; I am calm, untroubled and happy; I feel the presence of God; God is the truth and the life eternal; I have life eternal; My house is in order; I am simply leaving an earthly existence; My spiritual self is the most important part of who I am; I am blissful, happy and at peace with myself; I love all that I have ever known; I have lived a full happy life; It is a happy time of change for me; I know dying is a peaceful experience; My mind is quick and alert; I let the physical part of me finish its job; God and I have made our final preparations; We do not die rather we transcend to another life; I look forward to my transcendence; I am happy and at peace with myself; My life has been a thing of beauty; I have lived a full and complete life; I am at peace; I leave this life with a happy heart; I will watch over my loved ones in my new life.

CHILL OUT—ELIMINATE STRESS

There are no simple solutions to eliminating stress in your life. Most stress is caused by lifestyle problems, such as diet, exercise, smoking, jobs, family situations, and just life in general. Stress is the overall response of the body to any demand (pleasant or unpleasant) made upon it emotionally or physically. Stressors are any stimuli, real or imagined, that produce stress. The program gives you positive statements that will support most of the major areas that cause stress in your life. Since positive words will help create a different chemistry in the body, this one factor alone will move you toward eliminating stress.

I am at peace with myself; I am calm, cool and collected; I am in control of my life; I enjoy my relationships with my family and friends; I am a flexible person; The future is nothing but hopeful and exciting; I work in a peaceful environment; I choose to handle life's problems calmly; I delegate jobs and chores to other family members; I discuss family problems calmly and peacefully; I lead a healthy, productive life; I am thankful for all that I am; I am thankful for all my successes in life; I have a good family and good friends; My friends and family are supportive of me; I enjoy taking time to relax daily; I love to exercise daily; Exercising is a normal part of my day; I eat nutritionally balanced foods; I plan enjoyable activities every week; I like quiet time with myself; I leave my work at the office; I have a lot of energy; I love to plan my holidays; I like to be organized in my job; I ask for help when I need it; I like to reward myself in small ways; I like accepting others positive comments; Others help me solve problems that arise; I can always finish a job tomorrow; I like to communicate appropriately my concerns to others; I have a wonderful personal life; I have a wonderful professional life; I'll do what I can today and finish later; I sleep soundly at night; I enjoy a restful night's sleep; I am flexible in my job; I like complimenting other; I enjoy a humorous joke or story; I laugh and joke easily; I am a high energy person; I manage my money appropriately; I never spend more than I make; I watch my credit card spending; I pay my bills on time; I know exactly what my living cost are; I communicate with my spouse about monthly expenses; I budget money wisely; I have a nice savings plan; I save for annual vacations; I set and maintain priorities; I organize my time daily; I do what I need to do now; I say no when necessary; I enjoy relaxing while I drive; I have a should do, a must do and a want to do list; I follow the list I make daily; I accomplish a lot during the day; I have a peaceful, tranquil life; I like to balance my life accordingly; I make time for leisure activities; I say no to salespersons when it is appropriate; I ask my mate to help me around the house; I am an assertive person; I communicate my needs; I politely and assertively communicate to my boss; I relax and meditate daily; I take time every hour to relax and breathe deeply; I spend quality time with family members; I am a honest and sincere person; I live in a comfortable home; I am a flexible, open and enjoyable person; I like to see the funny side of life; Laughter helps me relax and enjoy life; I volunteer in community activities; I give hugs easily; I enjoy my calm, peaceful life.

HEALING—MIND AND BODY

We have mentioned that everything begins with a thought, including use of positive words to create a healing environment within our bodies. Our bodies (through millions of cells) are activated by our commands. The body and all its cells are powerful, natural healing mechanisms that are activated as we think and speak. This is an ideal program to go along with other approaches, such as weight and tobacco management, exercise, or sports. Actually, it should be included in any program you are undertaking.

I have a powerful healing force within me; I am activating my powerful healing force; Total health is a natural state for me; My body is a natural healer of itself; I feel better and better each day; My body is healing itself as I speak; I have a powerful immune system; My immune system is working right now; My body is a beautifully designed healing force; I am growing stronger and healthier; Every cell in my body is working in perfect harmony; All my cells work together giving me perfect health; I am in control of my own healing; My body naturally restores itself; I am better, stronger and healthier today; I have a full sense of balance in my life; I change my eating habits to help my body; I exercise to help my body; There is nothing imperfect in my body; My body is healing itself constantly; I have perfect health; I have perfect health and vitality; I am worthy of perfect health; I am worthy of joy, happiness and good health; My birthright is love and a healthy body; The power of my mind is infinite; Happy thoughts create a happy body; I have positive healthy thought patterns; My body supports and loves me; Every cell in my body is in excellent health; I give attention to healthy loving ways; My thymus responds to my healing image; I deserve abundant health; I focus on my healthy body; My mind and body are one; I live in harmony with myself; I look for the fun in life; I am healthy and full of life; I get good exercise and plenty of sleep; I nurture and pamper myself; I have the power to maintain good health; I eat foods that nourish me; My body loves good healthy foods; I am whole, perfect and complete in every way; I am whole, healthy and full of energy; I love my body; I am healing right now; I choose to express and choose a good healthy life; I am full of joy and peace; I enjoy who I am; I focus on positive experiences; I look for the fun in life; I am loving and forgiving; I have love, joy and perfect health; I am the master of my health; I have happy, loving thoughts about myself; I am calm, peaceful and healthy; I am my own best friend; I love and care for myself; I experience everyday to the fullest; I have positive loving thoughts; I live in the here and now; I deserve to reach all my life's goals; I have happy thoughts about my health; I honor and respect my life energy; Dynamic energy flows through me continually; My body has its own healing intelligence; I release the healing power of my body; I have and deserve abundant health; I have a strong will and live life to its fullest; I am open to the limited possibilities around me; I live a full and active healthy life; I enjoy the beauty of my body; I love myself more and more; I am unique; I am the only me that will ever be; I trust myself; I let my body heal itself; My body is healing itself as I speak; I sleep seven to eight hours of restful sleep nightly; I have the power to achieve good health and stay healthy.

DEPRESSION—CO ME BACK TO LIFE

Depression can be a serious mental disorder in which a person suffers long periods of sadness and other debilitating emotions. It can also be situational in nature and occur during periods of stress. Once the stress is eliminated, normal health continues. Approximately, 10 to 14 million people in the United States suffer from some level of depression. The program is for the individual experiencing situational depression or who is taking some kind of mild medication, either doctor prescribed or over-the-counter. It will act as a good supplementary program to go along with whatever activity or treatment you are using.

I love myself; I love who I am; Life is exciting and wonderful; I stay focused and enjoy life; I have a wonderful mind; I have a wonderful with an excellent memory; I make good decisions; I love the decisions I make in life; I love the choices I have made in my life; I sleep soundly and wake energized; I am highly motivated; I am highly energized and motivated; I am extremely motivated and love life; I am a healthy vivacious person; I laugh and smile a lot; I have wonderful feelings about life; I am a worthwhile person; I often ask others for help; I like being around other people; I value who I am; I love life; I am a kind and forgiving person; I love to pamper myself; I often think of sex; I have a normal sex drive; Life is all about living; I enjoy every aspect of my life; I am one of Gods beautiful creations; People love and care about me; I show love and caring to others; I am happy and loving all the time; I love being with myself; I love my work; I have a happy social life; I love being around people; I have a lot of friends; I take good care of myself; I am a caring and loving person; I care and love those around me; My spirits are always high; I enjoy life; Everyone likes who I am; I am accepted by all my friends; I radiate love and caring to everyone; I am physically and mentally alert; I am healthy mentally and physically; My body heals easily; I have a positive upbeat attitude; I eat the right foods and stay healthy; I am always calm and peaceful; Life is beautiful and I am living my dreams; I love who I am today and tomorrow; I am a successful person; I have success and prosperity in my life; I am reaching my goals; I am thankful for all that I am; Every day is a new wonderful beginning; Today is my day; I am living today to the fullest; I just love life and who I am; Tomorrow is always another day worth living; I am always relaxed and calm; I am at peace with myself; I am the most positive person you have ever known; I love life and life loves me; I have a lot of interesting outside activities; I am always looking for something new in life; I have kind, loving relationship with everyone; What I send out comes back to me; I send out love; I send out positive loving vibrations to everyone; I am a kind, loving and forgiving person; I forgive all that have ever harmed me; I am performing well above my abilities; I like who I am; I am close to my family; I love and care about all my family members; I look forward to this new day; Today is my day; I take care of myself and enjoy who I am; Life is so wonderful; I love living this wonderful life.

THE GRIEF PROCESS

When we have an emotional injury the body begins a process of healing. This process is as natural as the healing of a physical wound. Many do not realize that loss can be other than the loss of a loved one. Consider these possible losses as well—divorce, break-up from an affair, moving, menopause, retirement, leaving school before finishing, a failed business transaction, or even an amputation. Whatever concerns you and has a strong emotional impact can be considered a loss. This program is built around all of the identified steps of the grief process necessary for healing an emotional wound.

I am growing stronger each day; I have a lot of help; I am moving on; I am not alone in this world; I feel calm, peaceful, and happy; I am dealing with the past; I am a great and wonderful person; My mind and body are healing; I look forward to tomorrow; I am peaceful, and breathe slowly; I enjoy a restful night's sleep; I develop a plan and stick to the schedule; I laugh at my silly mistakes; I am slowing down and living; I love to touch and be touched; I have the love of caring friends; I am a comforting and nurturing person; I enjoy all of life; I love and care about myself; I am gentle with myself; I have a lot of fun activities planned; I am developing close friends; I like talking to a counselor; I eat nutritional foods; I like to pamper myself; I like to pray, meditate and contemplate; I have plenty of time to heal; I am the only me that will ever be; I like seeing a funny movie; I enjoy life to the fullest; Time helps me to heal; I am growing stronger and stronger each day; I live in the present moment; I forgive all who have ever hurt me; Life is nothing but positive; I feel good about myself; My dreams are healing me; I see the beauty in everything; I let go and live a good life; I am a better person now; I praise myself for my courage; I make all my own choices in life; I like making decisions and changing; I am working on my own self-improvements; I like developing new interests; It's ok to be me; Today is what counts; I stay focused and live for today; I like asking others for help; I am inviting new people into my life; I have the freedom to choose who I am; I appreciate who I am; I appreciate my new freedom; My happiness is up to me; I celebrate today; I move on and enjoy life; I am a creative person; I am creative and love life; I take action and live a good life; I am joining several new groups; I enjoy my privacy and solitude; I look forward to the future; I like helping others; I make plans to give service to others; I visualize a new me; I am a new me; I enjoy who I am every day; I have lifted my spirit to a new high; I allow myself to have sexual feelings; I have a healthy attitude about life; I do little favors for my friends; I plan and have a party for friends; I love who I am; I am a great person to know; People like who I am; I share my feelings with others; I have a lot of activities on Sunday; I like planning my days; I feel like I have been born again; I am building a new, better tomorrow; I like being alone with myself; All of life is flowing through me at this moment.

Career Improvement/Business Success Programs:

CAREER—HAPPINESS AT WORK

It seems that almost everyone complains about his/her job or career. Why do we experience such unhappiness in the work place? Most of our lives are spent earning money to get what we want out of life, so our jobs should be fulfilling. The person who is happy and loves his/her job tends to be the person who becomes more successful. This program is designed to help you achieve better job satisfaction and a more satisfying career.

I am happy in my work; I love my job; I am a caring employee; I help and encourage others in the work place; I balance work and the rest of my life; I feel appreciated at work; My talents are appreciated at work; I use my talents to the fullest at work; I am becoming better and better all the time; I am an invaluable employee; I am appreciated for my loyalty to my work; Working makes my life easier; I am a happy employee; I am stimulated at work; My talents are recognized at work; I work in a healthy atmosphere; I am satisfied with the money I get at work; I feel confident about my career; I am growing daily in my career; I look forward to my next career move; I look forward to going to work; My family supports my work; My work does not take away from my family; I get a sense of achievement from working; I separate work and family life; I am energized at the end of each work day; I work in a positive atmosphere; I create a positive attitude at work; People like who I am; I am productive at work; My work environment is fair; My job description is defined and fair; I spend just the right amount of energy at work; The rules and work expectations are clear and fair; I work in a comfortable work environment; I respect my abilities; I continue to grow in the work place; I communicate accurately at work; I continue to work on my interpersonal communication skills; Others find me easy to be around at work; I am always happy and content at work; I pace myself throughout the day at work; I feel competent at work; I have skills and talents that are unique. Expectations are clear and fair at work; I am an expert at what I do at work; I am always learning and improving at work; I am kept interested in my work; I am proud of the work I do; I am proud of my abilities and talents; I have ample time to finish my work; I am always caught up at work; I always finish my work on time; I love to go to work every day; The work place is an exciting place for me; Work makes my life more enjoyable; Work and the rest of my life are in perfect harmony; I always am precise in my work; I work with people I admire; People at work care about who I am; The people at work support me in my job; I look forward to improving my skills; I am growing and advancing in my job daily; I support my managers; My managers support me in my job; I have a satisfying relationship with all employees; I am a happy productive employee; Communicating is an important part of my job; I work overtime if necessary; I share positive work experiences with my family; I enjoy the benefits of working; I feel good about my choice to work in my present job; I choose to have a happy day at work; I am an expert at what I do at work; I am an invaluable person at work; Others see my unique talents and skills; I am easy to get along with at work; I have a lot of pride in my work; I respect my abilities in the work place; I admire the people I work with; Others admire and respect me at work; I am always fair and respectful to others at work; Others treat me with respect at work; I care about those in the work place; Others care about me at work; The positive energy I send out always comes back to me.

INTERPERSONAL SKILLS

To have a dynamic relationship with anyone you choose, you must learn to communicate at a deeper emotional level that will ultimately foster open communication with others. The program will help you become a receptive listener and unleash incredible feelings of self-confidence necessary to foster the kind of close relationships you so desire. You will gain a deeper understanding of others and the skills to achieve mutual caring at a higher level than ever before.

I am a powerful person; I respect myself and others; I have excellent manners; I give compliments easily; I am self assured about my dealings with others; I have excellent communication skills; I speak softly, gently with feeling; I project myself emotionally when I speak; I speak with assurance and authority; I easily accept compliments from others; I am an active attentive listener; I enjoy listening to others speak; I always tell the truth; I am a positive person with high integrity; I can say no when I need to; My words are powerful; I choose my words wisely before I speak; Others respect me for who I am; I always keep my thoughts focused when communicating; I am an excellent attentive listener; I enjoy a good conversation; I use humor when speaking; I am an attentive focused listener; I watch for non-verbal cues when communicating; I take turns when communicating; I listen carefully and let the other person speak; I am an effective listener and speaker; I say what I mean with clarity; I always ask questions when necessary; Asking questions helps clarify my understanding; I say how I feel tactfully; I stay honest and forthright; I am confident when speaking; I always present one idea at a time; I am assertive and direct when I speak; I honor and appreciate others opinions; I express my feelings honestly and with feeling; I answer all questions I am asked; I use appropriate body language; I agree in an appropriate manner; I present information accurately; I use the proper tone of voice when speaking; I take my time and give clarity when communicating; I know how and when to apologize; I speak softly but loudly enough to be heard; Others respect what I have to say; I respect what others have to say; I am a natural conversationalist; I like constructive suggestions; I like to think about what I like to say; Repeating and paraphrasing helps create understanding; I am happy and enjoy communicating; I acknowledge others point of view; I speak and my thoughts flow freely; I like expressing my opinions appropriately; Gestures help give my message clarity; I face the other person when communicating; I acknowledge the person with a smile and nod; My body language often expresses my feelings; I communicate clearly and to the point; My questions often serve as suggestions; I do not use the word WHY in my conversations; I use words the listener will understand; I am pleasant and confident when I speak; I stay focused on what the person is saying; I ask for clarification in a mannerly way; I am an excellent and attentive listener; I am positive and give constructive comments; I willingly give and receive compliments; I start emotional statements with "I feel"; The tone of my voice reflects my feelings; I use words appropriate to the listener; I am happy when I get along with others; I feel free to agree and disagree; My positive remarks make others feel good; I reply in a gently way to constructive suggestions; I am peaceful, calm and relaxed when I speak; I do not interrupt when another is speaking; I ask for clarity when I do not understand; It is my responsibility to clarify my interpretation; Positive feedback is important to give; My enthusiasm is reflected in my body language; I am clear and to the point when I speak; Humor is important in a conversation; Taking turns is an important communication skill; I often reflect back my thoughts to the speaker;

Sharing turns brings out clarity and purpose in communication; I listen attentively to what the other person is saying; I let the other person finish before I go on; I am gentle and patient when communicating; I let the conversation flow smoothly; I embrace the other persons ideas; I am learning while in the process of communicating; I am capable of excellent communication; I establish rapport easily with others.

SUPER LEARNER—IMPROVED LEARNING

Anyone who has trouble with any part of learning or the school environment can profit from this program. We all have negative thoughts about learning that create anxiety, frustration and anger. Propel yourself into a new dimension and begin to overcome the learning resistance that exists in your mind.

I learn quickly; I appreciate my abilities; I am an unlimited person; I schedule my time to study; I remember everything I hear; Studying is a pleasure to me; I am a quick learner; I know I have a lot of wisdom; I remember everything I read; I am thankful for my good mind; I read and study well; I take excellent notes during class; I have a high IQ; I am naturally intelligent; I am a good student a write well; I express what I know easily; I like learning and am very capable; I easily remember and retain what I learn; I feel happy about answering questions; I believe in myself; I see myself doing well in my studies; My mind is quick and alert; I easily understand what I study and read; I release all blocks to success; I see myself getting excellent grades; I have an excellent memory; I am able to do well in all my school studies; I feel happy and believe in myself; I like learning new materials; My memory is accurate and powerful; I easily remember details; I forgive others and myself for my past learning problems; I do well in all subject areas; I am aware and alert during my classes; I do well with facts and figures; I am a creative person; I understand everything I learn; Learning is exciting and fun; I have excellent reasoning ability; My mind is logical and organized; I enjoy school and learning; Tests are fun for me; I am relaxed during tests; I solve problems quickly on tests; I feel good about my life; I accept myself as a good student; My thinking is fast and precise; I think quickly on tests; I am ready for all kinds of success in school; I deserve to do well in school; I focus my mind with ease; I am relaxed while studying; I am energized by learning; I am creative and feel alert in school; I have good judgment and wisdom; I am an intelligent wise person; I learn quickly and easily; I have instant recall of facts; I am advanced in my learning ability; Nothing is too hard for me to learn; My IQ continues to go up daily; I am learning faster and faster each day; I like learning new subjects; Learning new subjects comes easy and natural for me; I read faster and remember more now; I have decided I will be a student for life; Life is exciting and I learn continuously; I remember everything I study; My memory is improving daily; I learn faster because I stay focused; People are amazed how quickly I learn; I remember everything I see; I have an excellent memory; My reading comprehension goes up easily; I have a lot of instant recall of facts; My memory is continually improving; The more I read the quicker I learn; My mind serves me well in all learning situations; My mind is powerful and energized; I remember and visualize stories easily; New concepts come easily for me; I am an unlimited person; I am articulate and knowledgeable; I am a student of life; I discover and learning comes natural for me; I am relaxed, calm and a quick study person; When I learn new information, I focus my attention; I learn faster because I am focused; All knowledge is available to me; Having an active mind keeps me youthful.

SELLING—SALES POWER

This is definitely a twenty one-day program. All the positive statements contained in the program are necessary and important to have engrained into your subconscious mind. The important topics, such as prospecting, making the presentation, overcoming objections, and enthusiasm, are contained in the program. The mental aspects of sales are far more important than the technical skills necessary to sell an item. One has to believe and have a strong self worth to overcome the excuses and doubt associated with selling.

I love to sell; Selling is for me; I am the best salesperson around; I am the best and getting better; I am always prepared to sell; I am always prepared to meet the public; I dress nicely and appropriately; I am a charming person; People like what I have to say; I have an upbeat attitude; I am kind and pleasant; I begin each day with enthusiasm and a clear mind; I develop a plan for each day; I always follow my plan and goals; I am a true professional; I have high integrity; I am hard working and organized; I attract people to me; I am highly successful; I love meeting and talking to people; I love meeting and selling people; I am hard working, and organized; I am energetic, enthusiastic and successful; I have a lot of energy; I am good at persuading others; Others like to be persuaded by me; I help people reach their goals when buying; I am a charming person to be around; I take time to do the right job; Customers are attracted to me; I service my customers well; Customers always return to me; I present good ideas and suggestions; I listen intensely; I am a good communicator; I take care of customers details; I am honest and friendly; People are attracted to me; I make a good sales presentation; I am always calm, cool and collected; I always smile; I am polite and smile a lot; I stay focused and centered; I am calm and peaceful; I present a state of calm during my presentations; My sales presentations are professional; My sales presentations are always effective; I handle all problems calmly; I keep working and winning; I deserve the sales I make; I am a capable productive individual; I am always honest and sincere; I can be trusted; I am skillful, trusting and determined; I ask for the order frequently; I like who I am; I have no hesitation about asking for the sale; I ask for the sale at each buying signal; I close, close, close; I begin closing from the beginning; I am always positive and upbeat; I get the most out of my time with a customer; I work hard at my profession; I set specific short and long range goals daily; My enthusiasm is contagious; I concentrate on the task at hand; I pay attention and stay focused; I enjoy and sell easily; I know all my products and services; My products and services are valuable; I give value in each contact I make; I believe in my products and services; I am always relaxed and in charge; My customers are valuable prospects; I prospect through my customers; I am a super-charged sales person; Each contact is a valuable opportunity; I believe in myself; I am a super star salesperson.

ORGANIZATION

Being organized is important in any endeavor in life, whether it be school, family, work, athletics, church or the multitude of activities in which you might be involved. Organizational skills are necessary to build a business, a career, family unit, relationships or any aspect of your life. Our universe is an organized place where we plant a seed of corn and corn grows. However, if we plant a seed in poor soil or do not water it, it does not grow. Paying attention to details in the organizational process is critical. This program is for anyone who wants to have a sense of being in control through organizational management.

I like being organized; I pay attention to details; I am organized and pay attention to details; I am organized and successful; My success and organizational skills go hand in hand; I allocate my energy wisely; I have time to organize; I lay out a plan for my day; I take time to organize my day; I plan and stay organized;

I plan my day and work my plan; I always have time during the day; I build accurate organized plans; I keep my work area organized; I organize my family life; I am totally organized and plan my day; I am successful because I am organized; I assure my success and stay organized; I organize and outline my personal goals; I tie my desires and goals together; I organize my goals daily; I allocate my time appropriately; I attain my goals through organizational skills; I fulfill my potential I am organized; I pay attention to my daily schedule; I work around my time frame; I am always right on time; I build a time log of daily activity; I evaluate my time and activities; I clarify what time I need for each activity; I have improved and managed my time accordingly; I am in control of my life; Time is a valuable resource; I record all my daily activities; I pay attention and shift my times accordingly; I set priorities and plan my day; I start planning around my priorities; I have a organized daily routine; I am at peace with myself; I always have a lot of energy to finish tasks; I have an organized day; I set time for relaxation and meals; I feel good about myself; I stay on task; I have good self-management skills; I have control over my work environment; I have control over my home environment; I have control over my life; I have written goals; I always make the right decisions; I have small manageable priorities; I meet my goals; I work my plan and follow my priorities; My time estimates are realistic; I always finish my defined tasks; Others help me with my goals; I am a team player; I can say no when needed; I have an organized social life; I am a patient person; I listen and pay attention to others; I have a lot of self-discipline; I have good communication skills; I take good notes and stay organized; My life is simple but organized; I effectively organize my life; I have a simple and happy organized life; I track my time and progress daily; I take time to reflect on my day; I honor others time; I pay attention to others tasks; My life is calm, peaceful and simple; I finish all my important projects on time; I make regular progress reports on my activities; I take time to evaluate my daily plan; I accept responsibility easily; I organize all my responsibilities; I delegate when necessary; I follow up on tasks I have delegated; I break my daily task into assignments; I enlist others help when necessary; I am working at top efficiency; I have clear priorities; I have short and long term goals; I balance my personal life and career; I set aside blocks of time; I develop a to-do list of activities; I stay focused and work my plan; I make appointments when necessary; My goals are written down; My goals are consistent and flexible; My goals are achievable; I have daily physical goals; I plan for educational improvements; I have financial goals.

Children's Programs For Adults:

DISCIPLINING MY CHILD

Designed as a reminder program, it touches on important concepts for parents during the child-discipline process. All parents and children face discipline challenges. Appropriate and consistent discipline makes life smoother and more pleasant for you, your child and everyone in the family. The goals covered are: to encourage appropriate behavior, to promote harmony in the family, to help the child cope with problems that arise as he/she grows up, and to help establish lifelong self-discipline. The program does not have to be used as a twenty-one (21) day program since a lot of the concepts do not have to be engrained into the subconscious. Use it as a reminder of what you need as a parent to discipline your children.

My child learns from example; I encourage appropriate behavior in my children; I love my children; I teach self-discipline to my children; Appropriate and consistent discipline is my goal; Good discipline now makes life smoother and pleasant; The family appreciates good discipline; My children become more self-reliant through good discipline; I teach my children to become responsible; I teach my children self control; Teaching respect for other is important; I have polite and kind children; I make sure my children are loved; My children respect others; Discipline is an ongoing process; Teaching respect for others is important; My children respect others belongings; I teach my children how to express their emotions; Teaching about feelings is important; I give my children praise; I give my children attention and love; I praise good behavior; I give attention to good behavior; I show my children how to care for themselves; I teach my children how to be orderly; I show my children how to develop good habits; I deliberately communicate with my children; I teach my children how to communicate; I understand my child's behavior; I talk to my children about their behavior; My children and I talk about appropriate behavior; I encourage appropriate behavior; I reward positive behavior; I reassure my children with love; I reassure my children with praise; I reassure my children with smiles; I listen carefully when my child speaks; I am consistent with my discipline; I show love to my children; I listen attentively when my children speak; I show interest when my children speak; I pay attention when my children speak; I have a special time each day to listen to my children; I work and play with my children; I set realistic limits; Realistic limits are necessary for safety; I share my reasons for setting limits; I repeat my limits when needed; I set limits on time management; I set limits on boundaries; I encourage appropriate behavior; I praise and reward for appropriate behavior; I smile, hug, kiss and thank my children for good behavior; I teach limits to promote independence; I start setting limits at birth; My children share in discipline decisions; We discuss emotions and their meaning; I set my own limits and stick to them; I am polite and reassuring to my children; I require my children to be polite to everyone; I develop work assignments for my children; I praise for tasks completed; I discipline out of love; I take action when necessary; I take action immediately; I am always firm, fair and consistent; My children and I agree on what behavior is expected; I value my children as individuals; I avoid spanking, hitting or punishing children; I control my emotions; I communicate with love; I understand my children's basic needs; I am clear and concise when I communicate; My discipline is a positive experience; My discipline is a continuing process.

Children's Programs (ages 4-12):

GOLFING FOR CHILDREN—CHASING THE LITTLE WHITE SPHERE

Golf is a challenging and individual sport that requires mental activity, even for children. Because golf is a thinking sport, golf rewards calm, patient players. This program is about developing strong mental skills, as well as basic skills that become habits. Having the mental and basic skills will make the game easier and more enjoyable. This is a twenty-one day program to engrain the basic concepts into the minds of the younger generation.

I am a great golfer; I love the game of golf; Golf is relaxing for me; I enjoy a game of golf; I take time and select the right club; I keep my eye on the ball; I am peaceful and tranquil; I am always calm, and cool; I am courteous on the course; Golf is fun and relaxing; I am perfecting my swing; I practice on the driving range; I perfect my skills with each club; I practice putting before each game; I am relaxed; I watch my breathing; I relax before each swing; I have a beautiful smooth swing; I have a smooth swing; I have a great follow through swing; Golf is fun and relaxing; I am always positive; I have a great attitude; I pay attention to the little details; I practice being consistent; I choose the proper position for each shot; I stay relaxed and focused; I study and pick the right club; I stay focused; I focus on each shot; I have courage; I am confident; I am mastering the game; Golf is challenging and fun; I am excited to do my best; I have many successes on the golf course; Golf is the greatest game invented; I find golf pleasant; I stay focused on one thing at a time; I have good rhythm in my swing; I use the proper hand position; Each shot is success; I control my emotions; I play the best shot; I enjoy making a good stroke; I work on improving my game; My golf swing is smooth; I have confidence in my swing; I am, calm and confident; I am calm and in control; I practice, practice, practice; The road to success is to practice; I am patience; I stay calm; I have a will to win; Every shot I take is perfect; I have a passion for the game; I trust myself to make the right decision; I love putting; The putting stroke is short and simple; I have a good feeling when I putt; I putt the ball smoothly; Golf is a peaceful sport; Golf is a rewarding sport; I have confidence.

SUPER LEARNER—IMPROVED LEARNING (YOUNG CHILD'S EDITION)

The program insures that children have healthy thoughts about school and learning. Any child who has trouble with any part of learning or the school environment will profit. Start propelling your child into a new dimension and help him/her overcome learning resistance.

I learn quickly; I like who I am; I am a super person; I am good at most things; I schedule my time to study; I remember everything I hear; Studying is a pleasure to me; I am a quick learner; I know I have a lot of wisdom; I remember everything I read; I am thankful for my good mind; I read and study well; I take excellent notes during class; I have a high IQ; I am smart; I am a good student and write well; I express what I know easily; I like learning and am very capable; I easily remember what I learn; I feel happy about answering questions; I believe in myself; I do well in my studies; My mind is quick and alert; I easily understand what I study and read; ; I get excellent grades; I have an excellent memory; I do well in all my school studies; I feel happy and believe in myself; I like learning new things; My memory is accurate and powerful; I easily remember details; I forgive myself for my past learning problems; I do well in all my subjects; I pay attention during my classes; I do well with facts and figures; I am a creative person; I understand everything I learn; Learning is exciting and fun; I have excellent reasoning ability; My mind is logical and organized; I enjoy school and learning; Tests are fun for me; I am relaxed during tests; I solve problems quickly on tests; I feel good about my life; I am a good student; I think fast; I think quickly on tests; I am successful in school;

I deserve to do well in school; I focus my mind with ease; I am relaxed while studying; I am energized by learning; I am creative and alert in school; I have good judgment; I am an intelligent person; I learn quickly and easily; I remember what I hear; Nothing is too hard for me to learn; My IQ continues to go up daily; I am learning faster and faster each day; I like learning new subjects; Learning new subjects comes easy for me; I read faster now; I will be a student for life; Life is exciting; I like learning; I remember everything I study; My memory is improving daily; I learn faster when I stay focused; People are amazed how quickly I learn; I remember everything I see; I have an excellent memory; My reading ability goes up easily; I have a instant recall; My memory is improving; The more I read the quicker I learn; My mind is alert; My mind is powerful; I remember stories easily; New things come easily for me; I can do whatever I want; I discover and learning comes easy for me; I am relaxed, and a calm child; I focus my attention; I learn faster when I pay attention; My mind is active all the time.

SELF ACCEPTANCE—I AM ME (CHILD EDITION)

When a child learns to be a positive being, he/she will have taken the first giant step to a rewarding and fulfilling life. Program your child's subconscious mind to believe in his/her self worth. Point him/her in a direction to achieve his/her potential.

I am a very special child; I live in the present moment; I am a warm and special child; I like life; I smile a lot; I am exciting and special; I am somebody important; I am a positive person; I love myself; I like who I am; I approve of who I am; I am a confident person; I am a lot of fun to be with; I am full of energy; I am a very intelligent person; I like other people; Other people like me; I am always full of life; I like how I feel and think; I am very special; I believe in myself; I make a difference; I have a lot of ability; I am honest; I am clever; I am strong; I feel good inside; I have good thoughts; I am proud to be me; I have a can do feeling; I feel sure of myself; I like who I am; I approve of who I am; I have talents and skills; There is a glow around me; I am so glad to be alive; I am a very special person; My mind is alert; I make things work for me; Others find me attractive; I am honest and genuine; I appreciate my strengths; I am a lovable child; I like who I am; I am in charge of my life; I am changing every day; People like to hear what I have to say; There is no one else like me in this world; My self confidence is awesome; I have a sense of excitement in my life; I have a lot of power; I feel good about myself; I love and appreciate myself; I have caring friends; I have beautiful personal qualities; I am a confident person; I have a can do attitude; Who I am makes a difference; I am the only me that will ever be; I appreciate all that I learn; I like all my blessings in life; I deserve everything I create; I have powerful inner strengths; I am an exciting child; Others find me easy to be with; Every day is a new exciting beginning; I allow others to get to know me; I am filled with positive self confidence; I deserve everything good in life; I have a lot of energy; I would rather be me than anyone else; Everywhere I go I go with love.

JUMP START YOUR DAY (CHILD'S EDITION)

When your child cannot muster up positive feelings due to difficult circumstances, help your child "jump start" the day. Use this program in the morning before starting the day. About four or five minutes into the program, a change will occur to alter feelings from negative to positive.

I spread around love; I am a positive caring person; I am a very happy person; My life is very friendly; Life is exciting; I relax and am very calm; I give and accept love; I like being active; I am at peace with myself; All is well, all is love; Love is the best gift I can give; I live today with joy; I am a positive person; I create my own future; I love school; I love life; I love my family; I love my friends; I radiate good health; I like who I am; I like to hug my parents; I trust myself; I am a powerful person; I choose my words wisely; I like listening to people talk; I am confident when I speak; I accept help into my life; I have power over how I think; I like change in my life; I have a happier way of life; I live a joyful, fun life; I have a zest for life; I am young and exciting; My life is carefree and simple; I care about myself; I am calm, and peaceful; Exercise is fun and enjoyable; What a lovely world I live in; I can change my feelings; I am a warm, and special child; I am a lot of fun to be with; I am a very special child; I like life; Everywhere I go I go with love; I have a peaceful life; I am successful; I welcome every day; I claim all my goodness; I am calm and peaceful; I laugh and smile easily; I like myself today; I am in control of my life; I love who I am; Good thing happen in my life; I am peaceful; I am loving; I accept my own personal growth; I deserve to be happy; I love and care for myself; Loving myself is good; I am kind and loving; I am a strong child; I enjoy life; I like good things in my life; I see all the beauty around me; I feel good about myself; Each day is a new blessing in my life; I am responsible for my own life; I control my own life; Life is exciting and fun; I trust, and respect myself; I am whole, and perfect; I have true self-love; I control my own feelings;

I choose how I feel; I like my abilities; I am a happy person; I am thankful for all my good; I am liked, and loving; Life is fantastic.

ENRICHING RELATIONSHIPS—(CHILD'S EDITION)

The program is good for helping children work on any kind of relationship, whether with parents, siblings or friends. Children will start living a happy, more secure life, filled with people they love.

I am a caring child; I radiate love; I accept others for who they are; Others accept who I am; I am a forgiving child; Others forgive me; I am a gentle loving person; I accept love easily; I bring loving people to me; I send out the feelings of love; I laugh easily; I like to smile and laugh; I am a joyful child to be around; I am a very trustworthy child; I am a loving child; I am a positive caring child; I am fun to be around; I am patient and kind; I am easily satisfied; I am a very happy child; I accept my parents; I trust my parents; I am honest with my parents; I am a good listener; I love my parents; Others care about me; My life is very happy; I am a very happy person; I am happy about my life right now; I live life to the fullest; I like others; I am kind to others; I am a fun child to know; Life is always good to me; I am open and receive love; I give love easily; Others love and trust me; I attract people to me; I am an honest child; I like to talk to others; I am a kind and gentle child; I am an easily satisfied and happy child; Others like me because I radiate love; I enjoy people of all kinds; I am a trustworthy and a positive child; I accept and forgive others; I can be loved by others; I am loving and affectionate; I give love and kindness to others; I respond to my parents requests; I am able to have rich relationships; I am a kind, strong and loving child; I listen well when others speak; I like receiving love from everyone; I love to hug my parents; I enjoy hugging others; I am loving and attract people to me; I receive much affection and love; I am a wonderful and kind child; My life is happy and full of joy; I like myself and others; Each day life gets better and better; I receive love easily; I am a kind and loving child; Others like to be with me; I am a child who attracts love; I am absolutely a loving child; I am a naturally loving and beautiful child; I have much love and caring from everyone; Others are kind and good to me I freely give my love; I am a good listener; I enjoy other children; I have good friends; I am known for my kindness; I love all people; I draw the best people to me.